in the days of thy youth

devotional readings for young people

WALTER DUDLEY CAVERT

Nashville   ABINGDON PRESS   New York

IN THE DAYS OF THY YOUTH

Copyright © 1971 by Abingdon Press

ISBN 0-687-19355-9

Library of Congress Catalog Card Number: 74-158674

Scripture quotations unless otherwise noted are from the
Revised Standard Version of the Bible, copyrighted
1946 and 1952 by the Division of Christian Education,
National Council of Churches, and are used by permission.

The poem by Rebecca McCann was taken from *Complete
Cheerful Cherub* by Rebecca McCann. Copyright © 1932 by
Covici Friede, Inc. Renewed 1960 by Crown Publishers, Inc.
Used by permission of Crown Publishers, Inc.

The poetry by Grantland Rice was taken from *The Final
Answer and Other Poems* by Grantland Rice. Used by permission of A. S. Barnes & Co., Inc.

The poetry by Christopher Fry was taken from "A Sleep of
Prisoners," by Christopher Fry. Copyright 1951 by Chris-
topher Fry. Reprinted by permission of Oxford University
Press, Inc.

SET UP, PRINTED, AND BOUND BY THE
PARTHENON PRESS, AT NASHVILLE,
TENNESSEE, UNITED STATES OF AMERICA

To
THE CHARLTON SCHOOL
Burnt Hills, N.Y.

PREFACE

Years ago I wrote a book of daily devotions for young people under the title *Remember Now*, which took its name from the opening words in a verse from Ecclesiastes, "Remember now thy Creator in the days of thy youth." It received such a favorable reception that at the publishers' suggestion I have written this little book as a sequel.

The title comes from the last words in the same Bible verse, *In the Days of Thy Youth*. It seeks to give practical guidance to daily Christian living in a changing and confused world where both young and old are often uncertain as to the course a Christian should follow.

Behind both books is the deep conviction that the problems of life in every generation can be adequately solved only in the light of the unchanging truths of the gospel of Jesus Christ.

Jesus is never out-of-date. He is so far ahead of us that we have not yet succeeded in catching up with him.

WALTER DUDLEY CAVERT

CONTENTS

A GREAT TIME TO BE YOUNG

SUNDAY—Week 1

√ **A GREAT AGE IN WHICH TO LIVE** Read Ps. 119:9-16

Remember now thy Creator in the days of thy youth.
—Eccles. 12:1 (KJV)

More than a century ago Arthur Cleveland Coxe, while a student for the ministry, wrote a poem which was set to music and is still found in our hymnals:

> We are living, we are dwelling,
> In a grand and awful time;
> In an age on ages telling
> To be living is sublime.

It sounds contradictory to call anything both "grand" and "awful," but the words were true in the era preceding the Civil War. And once more they can be accurately used in our own day. Man has been able to master the secrets of nature until he stands in awe before the possibilities of the future. If people make love the law of life and learn to work together as members of one family of God, the world can be made a Garden of Eden. At the same time, a selfish use of power can blast the world into bits, or pollute it until it is uninhabitable.

What a sublime privilege to be alive in such a day! It is a glorious time to be young.

"O God, as our knowledge of the universe increases, grant us the wisdom and courage to use it wisely."
—Astronaut John H. Glenn, Jr.

MONDAY—Week 1

IS THE SUN RISING OR SETTING?   Read John 1:1-8

Again Jesus spoke to them, saying, "I am the light of the world; he who follows me will not walk in darkness, but will have the light of life."—John 8:12

When the Constitutional Convention was held in Philadelphia after the close of the American Revolution, the sessions dragged on until many delegates despaired of being able to frame an instrument of government which all the colonies would approve. But at last the task was successfully completed. As the convention adjourned, Benjamin Franklin called attention to the chair in which George Washington had been sitting as chairman. Painted on its back were the streaming rays of a gilded half-sun. "I have been wondering," said Franklin, "whether that were a rising or a setting sun. Now I am sure that the sun is rising and that this is the dawn of a new day."

As one looks at the confused state of our present world, he may question whether the sun of civilization is rising or setting. The answer depends largely on whether the torch of Christian faith continues to spread its rays over our land.

The best in American life has grown out of the Christian convictions of our ancestors, and can be preserved only as the light of Christ is kept brightly shining. Jesus is still calling young people to follow him.

10

O God, help me to remember my Creator in the days of my youth. Take my life into your keeping and make me a worthy follower of your Son, Jesus Christ. Amen.

TUESDAY—Week 1

SLEEPING THROUGH A REVOLUTION
Read Eph. 5:6-14

Awake, O sleeper, and arise from the dead, and Christ shall give you light.—Eph. 5:14

Everyone is familiar with Washington Irving's story about Rip Van Winkle. After his long sleep of twenty years in the Catskill Mountains, he went back to his favorite tavern where he was surprised to see that the picture of King George III had been replaced by that of George Washington. Without knowing what was happening, poor old Rip slept through a revolution. World-shaking events had taken place. A new era had begun in history, but he had had nothing to do with ushering it in.

The story can be interpreted as a parable of contemporary life. The old world is passing away and a new world is coming into existence. Some people seem asleep to what is going on. They prefer to dream without being disturbed. Others are so afraid of the changes that they are hiding their heads under the bedclothes.

This is not a time to sleep or hide or run away. Thank God for the joy of living in stirring days, and ask him to show you how you can make your life count in the biggest way.

Stab me awake, O God, to the greatness of the days in which I am living. Lead me into a clearer understanding of your purpose for the world and your will for my life. In Jesus' name. Amen.

11

WEDNESDAY—Week 1

✓SEEKING THE BEST   Read 1 Cor. 12:27-31

Earnestly desire the higher gifts.—1 Cor. 12:27-31

A handsome youth by the name of Plato was walking down a street in Athens when he met a baldhead named Socrates. "Where can I find the best things in life?" asked the older man. Plato was surprised that a person of middle age did not know where to find the shops that sold the best food and wine. Then Socrates, without waiting for an answer to his first question, asked another, "What are the best things?" This was the beginning of a long discussion which resulted in a lasting friendship. It opened the eyes of Plato to the higher values of life, and changed his future.

The question asked by Socrates needs to be raised with young people in every generation. How often people miss the best! They mistakenly suppose that if they can get money enough, they can buy the highest satisfactions of life. They fail to realize that true riches are found only in the realm of the spirit.

Life was never the same for Plato after meeting Socrates. It will never be the same for anyone who wrestles seriously with the question of what deserves his highest loyalty.

Dear God, keep me from being satisfied with second best. May I have the faith to believe that if I give you first place in my life, the other things which I need will be supplied through the richness of your love. Amen.

THURSDAY—Week 1

WE MUST BE THE WORLD WE WANT
Read Matt. 7:13-20

Every sound tree bears good fruit, but the bad tree bears evil fruit.—Matt. 7:17

12

The world of tomorrow is rushing in upon us. We hope it will be a better world, but amid all the changes one fact is basic. Society is made up of individuals. Each person must fulfill his longings by making his own particular contribution to society. We must be the world we want.

Do we wish a world of beauty? Then we must beautify the place where we live. Do we want a world of truth and honesty in which nations will keep their pledges to each other? Then integrity must be in the hearts of its people.

A convict once broke out of jail to visit his daughter. She had been writing cheerful letters telling her father how well she was getting along. The father, however, suspected that she was concealing the actual facts. He found that his worst fears were true. The girl was living in desperate want. The father told her this was no reason for deceit. His own downfall, he said, was due to a lack of inner integrity, and he urged her to be honest and truthful in all of her relationships.

Do you want a new world? Then start to make your own life new.

Dear Father, help me to make my life the channel through which truth and love will flow out into the life of mankind. For Christ's sake. Amen.

FRIDAY—Week 1

ANSWERING THE CALL OF GOD   Read Jer. 1:1-8

The Lord said to me, "Do not say, 'I am only a youth' . . . for I am with you."—Jer. 1:7-8

Many young people have a sense of frustration and helplessness. They live in a world of baffling problems but feel powerless to do anything about them. They

13

are like Jeremiah, who lived near Jerusalem at a time when the future of Israel was dark. Babylon and Egypt were fighting for world mastery, and it looked as though Israel would inevitably be drawn into the fray. It might mean that Israel would be crushed forever.

Jeremiah heard God calling him to do something to prevent such a disaster. He gave the answer which youth are apt to give today, "I am too young; what can I do?" God replied: "Do not say that. Be not afraid. I will be with you." Jeremiah responded to the call and became the greatest leader of his day. He did not prevent the Israelites from being carried into exile, but he kept alive their faith and hope so that it later was possible for them to return to their own country.

He was not as helpless as he thought he was. No one is helpless if he seeks help from God. In every situation there is something one can say or do that may be creative.

Save me from discouragement, O God. Guide me by thy spirit that I may find the way in which I can best serve thee. Then give me the courage to go bravely forward. Amen.

SATURDAY—Week 1

NOW IS THE TIME TO DECIDE   Read Mark 1:16-28

Jesus said to them, "Follow me" . . . . And immediately they left their nets and followed him.—Mark 1:17-18

An old legend tells how an angel appeared to a boy who was chasing butterflies. "You should be preparing to do the work of the Lord," said the angel, "he needs people who will help him in his effort to make a better world." "I know it," replied the lad, "but just now I am playing and enjoying my childhood."

Soon the boy was a teenager. The angel passed by again. "Have you begun the Lord's work?" he asked. "Not yet," answered the youth, "but I will when I have finished my fun." The angel came again when the youth had grown to middle age. "Are you laboring in the Master's vineyard?" he inquired. The man turned his eyes away and said: "Soon I will be, but first I must make money for myself." Later the angel met an old man tottering toward an open grave. "Did you finish the work God gave you to do?" he asked. "Alas, no," was the reply, "but now the night has come, and it is too late."

Do you have some high goal you hope to achieve? Now is the time to begin. Notice that Mark describes the disciples as people who acted immediately.

Dear Heavenly Father, keep me from putting off until tomorrow what I ought to do today. Make me a person of decision and action. Amen.

FINDING OUT WHO I AM

KNOW YOURSELF Read Ps. 8

What is man that thou art mindful of him? . . . Thou hast made him little less than God.—Ps. 8:4-5

On a rocky crag above a Grecian sea stand the ruins of the old temple of Apollo in Delphi. Inscribed on the marble is a quotation from Socrates, "Know thyself." These words have stirred the thinking of people for over two thousand years, but were never more challenging than today. With all his modern knowledge, man is still not sure of his identity.

An exhibit of modern art included a painting in which one could see three different pictures, depending on the angle from which he viewed it. If you stood directly in front and gave a long straight look, the picture was clearly that of a man. If you moved a little to one side, where you had a slanted viewpoint, the likeness was that of an animal. Seen from the other side, the picture changed to that of a machine.

The artist was trying to say that many people look at man from the wrong angle. They have a slanted viewpoint and conclude that man is less than a human being. The most satisfying description is that of the Psalmist, who gave a searching

16

look at the whole universe and called man the climax of creation, surpassed only by God.

Take the veil from my eyes. O God, that I may behold the spiritual nature of the universe. Help me to know myself as a child of God. Amen.

MONDAY—Week 2

THE MYSTERY OF ME　　　　　Read Gen. 1:26-31

So God created man in his own image.—Gen. 1:27

"Poor guy, he never knew who he was." These are the closing words in Arthur Miller's play, *Death of a Salesman.* They form an accurate summary of the lives of countless people who drift through life without ever facing the basic issue about themselves.

"Who am I?" Every serious-minded person must ask himself this question. Am I a chance collection of atoms? Am I related only to the physical world, or is there something about me that links my life to that of God?

In the Genesis story, God created the earth and saw that it was good. Out of the dust of the earth he then created man. But he also breathed into him his own spirit and made him in the divine likeness. Man is thus a mixture of dust and divinity. Man is a part of the physical creation, but that is not all. He is made in the image of God and is able to think and know and love.

The Greek word for man is *anthropos.* Its literal meaning is "an upward-looking animal." Though man is an earthly creature, he has a lifted head and is capable of communion with his Creator.

Eternal Father, help me to understand who I am. May I never forget that I am loved by you and intended for fellowship with you. Amen.

TUESDAY—Week 2

MY EXCUSE FOR BEING BORN   Read 1 John 4:7-13

For this was I born, and for this I have come into the world, to bear witness to the truth.—John 18:37

Children in the first grade of a certain school were asked to bring their birth certificates and show them to the teacher. The next day a little girl stood crying outside her classroom door. When the teacher asked her what the matter was, she said: "I lost my excuse for being born."

Surely it is a cause for deep concern if we have lost our reason for being on earth, or if we have never discovered why we are here! Life is meaningless and empty until we can give an adequate reason for our existence.

"For this was I born," said Jesus, "to bear witness to the truth." He knew what he was living for. He wanted to help people understand that God is love, and to show what it meant to apply that basic idea to all the varied relationships of life.

This is also the mission of every Christian—to go out into the world of hate and misunderstanding and show what life means when it is lived in the spirit of Christlike love.

Grant, O God, that I may fulfill the purpose for which you have sent me into the world. Each day may I seek to reflect the spirit of Christ. May there be more love in the world because I have lived. Amen.

WEDNESDAY—Week 2

LEARNING TO WHOM WE BELONG   Read Ps. 42

My soul thirsts for God, for the living God. When shall I come and behold the face of my God?—Ps. 42:2

During the Second World War, a French soldier was found standing in a railway station saying: "I don't know who I am but I want to go home." Because of the terrible experiences through which he had passed, he had a bad case of amnesia. Government officials put his picture in the paper, and three different families claimed him as their own. His face had been disfigured and treated by plastic surgery, so that his own relatives were not sure of his identity.

He was taken to the three villages where the families lived and allowed to walk around by himself. In the first two communities he wandered aimlessly, but in the third a gleam of recognition came into his eyes as he walked down the main street. He turned into a side street, walked up the steps of his home, and entered his father's arms.

Perhaps we are not sure to whom we belong and we also yearn to find our Father. The Psalmist tells how a man found God when he joined those going to the sanctuary. It will help us to recognize God as our Father if we join those who are worshiping him.

You are ever seeking me, O God. May I be willing to fulfill the conditions that make it possible for me to know you and be found by you. Amen.

THURSDAY—Week 2

THE VALUE OF A MAN Read Matt. 12:9-14

Of how much more value is a man than a sheep! —Matt. 12:12

A generation ago a chemist estimated that the elements in the human body were worth a little less than a dollar. On that basis man seemed cheap and trivial. More recently a magazine article reported that the increased cost of chemicals now make a man worth $34.50. His physical value has increased tremendously.

One of the costliest elements in the body is potassium. A person weighing 150 pounds must have four ounces. The body also contains three pounds of calcium phosphate, or enough to whitewash a good-sized chicken coop. In addition, there is enough carbon to make 9,000 pencils, enough phosphorus for 2,000 matches, enough fat for seven large cakes of soap, enough iron for a small nail, and sufficient magnesium for a dose of salts.

Is this all there is to a human being? Then he is indeed insignificant. The glory of man is that he is infinitely more than the materials of which he is composed. His body is directed by a mind which can think and love. And for this there is no adequate explanation, except an eternal Mind who made man in his own likeness.

Dear Father, help me to remember my value in your sight. Teach me that my true self is my best self. Grant that I may never think meanly of myself lest I dishonor you. In the name of Christ. Amen.

FRIDAY—Week 2

FOLLOWING GOD'S DIRECTIONS Read John 13:1-15

I have given you an example.—John 13:15

A man received a Christmas present which came in a box from Sears, Roebuck and Company. The gift was an object divided into sections which needed to be assembled. When he tried to put the parts together, the man found himself in a dilemma. Then he discovered in the box a card containing the manufacturer's instructions. On it were the words "when all else has failed, follow the directions."

Is not this a good suggestion for handling the life which comes to us as a mysterious gift from the Creator? When we try to develop it according to our own ideas, we are often unable to solve the problem. We need to go back to the instructions of the God who made us. In order that we might know his plan for us, God has given in Christ a revelation of what man ought to be, and by divine help can become. In the first four books of the New Testament, we have the record of his life and teachings.

When we are baffled and discouraged in our efforts to be what we would like to be, we can turn to the Bible for God's plans.

We thank you, O God, for Jesus Christ. Make us dissatisfied with ourselves as we are and help us to become more like him. In his name. Amen.

SATURDAY—Week 2

MAN'S GREATNESS AND HIS LITTLENESS
Read Matt 23:1-12

Whoever exalts himself will be humbled.—Matt. 23:12

The biblical idea of man emphasizes his greatness, but it also insists that he is dependent on God. We are his creatures. We did not make ourselves. Since we do not come into the world of our own choosing, we have no right to claim that we are free to do as we please. No matter how hard we try to control our own lives, we must someday give them up.

One of the great sins of modern man is that he insists on being his own god. We are like the ancient people on the plain of Shinar who tried to build the

21

Tower of Babel reaching up to heaven. They wanted to sit on the top of the world and to eliminate their dependence on anyone but themselves.

Because we are God's creatures, we can never be fully ourselves until we enter into a right relationship with him. Trying to defy God may bring a temporary thrill, but in the end it brings unhappiness. St. Augustine was speaking a great truth out of his own experience when he said, "Thou hast made us for thyself, O God, and we are restless until we rest in thee."

Dear Father, keep us from thinking more highly of ourselves than we ought to think. Make us willing to do your will. In Jesus' name. Amen.

HOW MATURE AM I?

SUNDAY—Week 3

MATURITY IS NOT A MATTER OF AGE

Read Heb. 11:23–12:2

Let us run with perseverance the race that is set before us, looking to Jesus, the pioneer and perfecter of our faith.—Heb. 12:1-2

A cartoon by Jules Feiffer shows a dignified gentleman stopping to talk to a youth who is carrying a sign. The gentleman says loftily: "I'll tell you what really bothers you kids today, YOU JUST DON'T WANT TO GROW UP!" The youth replies: "I once wanted to grow up, but then I took a look at the grown-ups around me. Mister, to my generation, NOT wanting to grow up is a sign of maturity."

No one can blame young people for not wanting to be like many of the adults who seem to have no higher purpose than to make money and spend it on self-centered living. But the fact that people are childish is no reason why anyone should remain that way.

Maturity is not a matter of age. A person can be young and mature. He can be old and immature. You do not become grown-up by being old enough to vote or to drive.

A person is mature when he has a sense of mission, can patiently face obstacles without being discouraged, stand up for his convictions, and sacrifice the present to the future.

Forgive me, O God, when I am restless and impatient. May it be my goal to do your will now and throughout all the years of my life. Amen.

MONDAY—Week 3

LIVING IN A HALL OF MIRRORS   Read 1 Pet. 5:1-6

You must all clothe yourselves in humility toward one another, for God opposes the proud, but shows mercy to the humble.—1 Pet. 5:5-6 (Goodspeed)

In the palace of Versailles is a room known as the Hall of Mirrors. Wherever you stand and whichever direction you look, you will see yourself. Some people live permanently in that kind of room. They are so immature they cannot see beyond their own immediate concerns.

Not long ago the daily papers carried an item about a woman who made a will in which she left her paintings to a museum which refused to accept them. Their reason was that she was the subject of each of the paintings. She had artistic talent, but used it only in an effort to glorify herself. She spent so much time gazing into the looking glass that her work had no attraction for other people.

How many times a person of fine abilities uses them in such a selfish way that he finds no personal happiness, and makes no lasting contribution to society.

A Greek legend tells about Narcissus, a handsome youth who saw himself reflected in a pool of water. Entranced with what he saw, he could not turn away. The more he looked, the more he wanted to look. Gradually he pined away until the gods took pity on him and changed him into a beautiful flower which could be a source of joy to those who saw it. This is the true beauty of life: to bring joy into the hearts of others.

Grant, O God, that the mirror of my self-admiration may be turned into a window through which I see the people who need my help. As I look out upon life, may I have Jesus' spirit of compassion. Amen.

TUESDAY—Week 3

THE NEED FOR PREPARATION   Read Matt. 25:1-13

Those who were ready went in with him to the marriage feast.—Matt. 25:10

From ancient Greece comes the legend about Phaëthon, the son of Helios, who drove the chariot of the sun. The boy asked for permission to guide the chariot and was as persistent as the modern youth in asking for his father's car. The permission was finally granted, but the fiery steeds were too unruly for the inexperienced driver. The horses carried the sun chariot so close to the earth that the ground was scorched and the rivers became dry. People cried out to Jupiter for relief and the great god reluctantly hurled a thunderbolt that killed the youthful charioteer. Ovid says that the following inscription was put on his tombstone:

He could not rule his father's car or fire
Yet it was much to so nobly aspire.

Youth are to be commended for their dreams and aspirations, but they must not allow confidence in their own abilities to take the place of training and preparation. In the parable of the wise and foolish virgins, Jesus said that only those who made adequate preparation were admitted to the marriage feast. The others found that the door was shut.

Grant, O God, that I may never be shut out from a great opportunity because I have failed to prepare myself. Help me to be ready for whatever life may bring. In Jesus' name. Amen.

WEDNESDAY—Week 3

AWAY WITH THE MANGER   Read Eph. 4:11-16

So shall we all at last attain . . . to mature manhood. We are no longer to be children.—Eph. 4:13-15 (NEB)

One of the sentimental aspects of the Christmas season which has special appeal is that it centers around the baby Jesus. It is easy to rhapsodize about a baby in a manger with hovering angels singing songs of heavenly glory. Even those who have made no serious effort to follow Jesus will join in the songs about the Bethlehem infant.

What we need to remember every day of the year is that Jesus did not remain a baby. He grew up to be the determined man who challenged the world's evil and injustice. He drove the moneychangers out of the temple because they were corrupting its worship and cheating the people. He denounced the Pharisees as hypocrites and children of the devil, because they were concerned about keeping the details of the Jewish ceremonial law but were indifferent to the demands of justice for the poor and oppressed.

Jesus told his followers that they must be willing to be unpopular and persecuted and that greatness consisted in service. He himself gave the example of sacrificial living and finally died on the cross.

26

A Christian has no right to sing about the manger unless he is willing to face the cross.

Make me willing to serve you, O God, without counting the cost. Instead of lingering long before the manger, may I kneel before the cross. For Christ's sake. Amen.

THURSDAY—Week 3

THE MATURITY OF JESUS　　　　Read Luke 2:41-52

Jesus increased in wisdom and in stature, and in favor with God and man.—Luke 2:52

We know but little about the boyhood of Jesus, but we have one significant verse which says that he grew not only in wisdom and stature but in favor with God and man. He became a fully developed individual.

Contrast that description of Jesus with the words which the prophet Hosea used about Ephraim, which is another name for Israel. "Ephraim is a cake not turned." In Palestine a common article of food was a little flat cake which was cooked on hot stones. It needed to be turned and cooked on both sides. The prophet said that his nation was a race of people who were only half-baked. They were cooked on one side but raw on the other. How many people are like that! They lack a well-rounded development which includes the moral and spiritual life.

Everyone feels sorry for a person whose physical development has been arrested so that he is left a dwarf. Much more pathetic is the person who has never developed an adequate sense of duty to God and man. He may be tall and smart and handsome, but something vital is lacking.

Grow up! Avoid being only half-baked.

27

We thank you, O God, for the revelation of perfect manhood in Jesus Christ. May the Christian life become my goal. In his name. Amen.

FRIDAY—Week 3

MATURITY REQUIRES STEADFASTNESS

Read Luke 9:57-62

No one who puts his hand to the plow and looks back is fit for the kingdom of God.—Luke 9:62

One of the sure evidences of maturity is the ability to work steadfastly for an unselfish goal in spite of all discouragements. In the movie based on the life of Madame Curie and her achievement in isolating radium, which became a cure for cancer, her husband gives up in despair. They have performed 487 experiments and seemingly without success. Pierre Curie strides across the room and says vehemently: "It can't be done. It can't be done. Maybe in a hundred years it can be done, but never in our lifetime." He turns to pace the floor again and meets the resolute face of his wife. She says: "If it takes a hundred years it will be a pity, but I dare not do less than work for it as long as I live."

The Christian is always faced with a task that seems impossible. He is seeking to establish a kingdom of love in a world dominated by hate and greed. Whether it takes a hundred years or a thousand, we must work for it as long as we live. For we follow a Lord who clung to his mission of brotherhood until, in the agony of the cross, he said, "It is finished."

O God, I thank you for the steadfast courage of Christ who refused to turn back from his high aim even though it cost his life. Give me the grace to follow him as my Master and my Friend. Amen.

28

SATURDAY—Week 3

GROWTH THROUGH A GREAT LOYALTY

Read Matt. 10:34-39

He who finds his life will lose it, and he who loses his life for my sake will find it.—Matt. 10:39

A former university dean, after being adviser to thousands of students, said the sign that a young man had emerged from his childhood lay in the discovery of some enterprise concerning which he says: "I belong to that." He becomes mature when he finds something beyond himself that lays claim upon his loyalty.

Most young people begin to feel grown-up when they can say, "This television set or this car belongs to me." They measure life by what they can accumulate and control. From the Christian standpoint, such an attitude betrays one's immaturity.

Think of the people who are admired in history. Each represented some cause to which he gave unswerving loyalty. The name of George Washington stands for American independence. Lincoln stands for freedom of the slaves. Martin Luther stands for religious liberty, and Martin Luther King for racial justice.

Every person can be devoted to some cause greater than himself. This is what makes a person grow and gives life higher meaning. Said George Bernard Shaw: "The true joy of life is being used for a purpose recognized by yourself as a mighty one."

O God, give me the kind of loyalty that will lift me above all littleness and make life worth living. May I have a great love for a great cause. For Christ's sake. Amen.

UNLOCKING MYSELF

SUNDAY—Week 4

THE KEY IS ON THE INSIDE   Read 1 John 4:13-21
Perfect love casts out fear.—1 John 4:18

Lewis Carroll, the author of *Alice in Wonderland,* once wrote a fantastic little story about the lock which had no key. It kept going to different people and saying, "I am looking for someone to unlock me." The story is a parable. Many people seem unable to release the abilities that dwell within them. Held back by a sense of inadequacy or a fear of failure, they lack the courage to tackle their problems. The doors of their personalities are locked so tight that they do not easily open.

The key that opens the door to a larger life is always on the inside. Other people can help you, but the final solution of your problem is within yourself. But how? By inviting Christ to come into your life. Let his spirit of love flood your soul and your fears will be washed away.

Think of what happened in the lives of people who became friends of Jesus and allowed him to "unlock" them. Take John, for instance, whose life was so self-centered that he once asked to be given a chief place in the new kingdom which he hoped Jesus would establish. In the end he became known as the apostle of love.

O God, you are ever outside the door of my heart, quietly knocking for admission. May I open the door and bid you to come in. Amen.

MONDAY—Week 4

THE VICTORY OF THE SPIRIT   Read Isa. 40:27-31

The Spirit helps us in our weakness.—Rom. 8:26

Young people are often depressed by the discovery of their limitations. Seeing others who are more talented or who get better marks in school. They decide that they themselves can never be a big success. Feeling frustrated, they no longer try. The first step toward self-confidence is self-acceptance. If you accept your situation without self-pity, you can make your limitation or handicap a spur to success.

If you are ever in Saranac Lake, New York, stop before the monument of Edward Livingstone Trudeau. On its pedestal is inscribed the single word "acquiescence." As a young doctor in Brooklyn, Trudeau became ill with tuberculosis and went to the mountains for his health. When he recovered, he was advised by other doctors that his best chance for continued health was to stay in the Adirondacks. Becoming deeply concerned about helping other people who were afflicted with tuberculosis, he built a hospital and became a pioneer in helping to overcome the disease. Happiness and professional success crowned his career.

In his autobiography, Trudeau speaks of "the victory of the spirit over the body." That is a victory we all can win.

Dear Father, grant that the power of your Spirit working within me may turn my weakness into strength and make me a useful servant in your kingdom. Amen.

TUESDAY—Week 4

DEVELOPING FAITH IN YOURSELF

Read 1 Cor. 9:15-23

As a man thinketh in his heart, so is he.—Prov. 23:7 (KJV)

How can one acquire faith in himself? One answer to the question is in the words of William James, a noted psychologist: "If you want a quality, act as if you already have it."

The truth of the statement is illustrated in the life of a man who in his youth was a minor league ballplayer. An old time professional watched his playing and later gave him some advice. "You have real ability," he said, "but you will never get ahead in baseball unless you have some enthusiasm." The young man protested that enthusiasm was not something you could turn off and on at will.

"You can make yourself act enthusiastic," the old pro replied. "It's as simple as that. Play with enthusiasm and soon you will have it." The young man decided to try it. He went into his next game as though charged by an electric battery. When he threw the ball, or ran, or batted, he did it with verve and energy. The next morning the newspaper referred to him as a human dynamo. Soon he was spotted by a scout for a major league and was playing in big-time baseball.

Make me enthusiastic, O God, over the highest and best things of life. Help me to begin now to find the joy of doing your will. In Jesus' name. Amen.

WEDNESDAY—Week 4

ONE WAY TO ELIMINATE FEAR

Read 2 Sam. 12:1-15

Be sure your sin will find you out.—Numbers 32:23

The person who would lead a fearless and confident life must guard his own integrity. Do something of which you are ashamed and you will be in constant dread of exposure. Make an unkind remark about some acquaintance and the next time you meet him, you will be afraid he knows what you have said.

In the Genesis story, Adam hid himself after he had eaten the forbidden fruit. This is not merely an old biblical tale. It is as modern as the morning newspaper. A man does wrong and then goes into hiding for fear his deed will become known. It is the experience described by Coleridge after the Ancient Mariner had killed the albatross:

> Like one that on a lonesome road
> Doth walk in fear and dread,
> And having turned around, walks on
> And turns no more his head;
> Because he knows a frightful fiend
> Doth close behind him tread.

Do you want to go through life unafraid? One essential is a clean and upright life, with no Bluebeard's closet which you dread to have opened.

Dear Father, keep me from the actions which afterward cause sorrow and shame. Grant that my conduct may be worthy of your approval and that I may never be a disappointment to my best self. Amen.

33

HOW A MOVIE STAR OVERCAME SHYNESS
Read Luke 9:23-27

Whosoever would save his life will lose it; and whoever loses his life for my sake, he will save it.—Luke 9:24

Jane Wyman, who became a Hollywood star, has told about her long fight against shyness. As a child, her only solution to her problem was to keep by herself. She said, "I was a well-mannered little shadow who never spoke above a whisper."

Then came the necessity to earn a living. Since her home was near Hollywood, she was able to secure a chorus part in the movies, but the work was agony. She put on a bold exterior but this did not change her inner attitude. She succeeded in getting more desirable roles but failed to solve her problem. Finally she talked to an understanding priest. She told him that she had thought her shyness would disappear if she could only succeed at something, but that in spite of considerable success, she felt just the same.

"Of course you do," said the priest. "Shyness isn't a matter of doing well or not doing well. It is a matter of self-centeredness." He gave her suggestions about becoming interested in others. Following his advice, she discovered "a whole world full of other people." Becoming concerned with their joys and problems, she forgot about herself.

"Best of all," she said, "I am finding God."

Dear God, open my eyes to the needs of others. Help me to learn that the person who becomes completely wrapped up in himself will make a small bundle. Make me bigger than my little self. Amen.

TIMID TIMOTHY　　　　　　　Read 2 Tim. 1:7

God did not give us a spirit of timidity, but of power and love and self-control.—2 Tim. 1:7.

One of the most effective leaders in the first century Christian church was a young man who had to overcome his natural timidity. When Paul sent Timothy on a mission to the church in Corinth, he wrote a special letter to members of the congregation. "When Timothy comes," he said, "see that you put him at ease among you. Let no one despise him."

Evidently the young minister was not the kind of person who could make an immediate impression on others. He was bashful and found it difficult to appear before a congregation.

Paul also wrote a letter to Timothy in which he dealt with this lack of confidence. He reminded him that "God has not given us a spirit of timidity, but of power and love and self-control." Here is a suggestion to help overcome self-distrust. Remember that your timidity does not come from God. He wants you to be unafraid.

If you are habitually shy, it is not because this is God's purpose for you. The attitude is one you have developed by allowing negative ideas to dominate your mind. Center your thoughts on God and not on yourself. Ask him to make you a source of help to other people.

O God, you are the one who can take away my discouragement and fearfulness. Help me to offer my life to you. Give me the strength I need to do a useful work in your kingdom. Amen.

35

THE SELF-CONFIDENCE OF JESUS

Read Luke 12:1-7

Do not fear those who kill the body, and after that have no more that they can do.—Luke 12:4

Did you ever stop to think about the self-confidence of Jesus? His background might normally have made him a timid soul. He was brought up in a village with such a poor reputation that Nathanael said, "Can any good thing come out of Nazareth?" Belonging to a peasant background, Jesus had no chance for special training as a rabbi.

But how boldly he faced the situations of his day! He was undaunted by the criticism of the Pharisees and the opposition of the officials in Jerusalem. It became evident that if he went forward in his chosen course, he would end on the cross. Even death could not stop him.

Where did Jesus get such a courageous attitude? For one thing, he was sure of his own integrity and singleness of purpose. In the second place, he was deeply concerned for other people. And in the third place, he had put his life completely in the hands of God. Add up these qualities that stood out so plainly in the life of Jesus—personal integrity, concern for others, and dedication to God. The sum total makes a fearless and confident soul.

Father, I thank you for the continued inspiration that comes to me through studying the life of Christ. Give me the desire to be more like him. In his name. Amen.

TEMPTATIONS UPWARD

JESUS THE TEMPTER   Read Matt. 16:13-20

I, when I am lifted up from the earth, will draw all men to myself.—John 12:32

"One of the strangest marvels in history," said Harry Emerson Fosdick, "is the way Jesus has tempted mankind. Whoever would have dreamed it? Alexander, Caesar, Napoleon—they might tempt us, making us wish we had power like theirs; but Jesus, born in a manger, dying on a cross, his message love, humility, goodwill—why should he tempt the race? Yet he is the greatest tempter mankind ever faced. We cannot get rid of him."

The fact that one knows Christ as he is portrayed in the New Testament is a challenge that cannot be lightly dismissed. If you once catch sight of him in all his strength and beauty, you will never be satisfied until you respond to his appeal and try to pattern your life after his. We usually think of the tempter as the devil, who seeks to draw us down the pathway of evil, but Jesus makes goodness and love so alluring that he beats the devil at his own game.

You can call Jesus an impossible idealist and make fun of him, but one thing you cannot do. That is to ignore him. He towers so high above us that you can never turn your eyes away. In your best moments you will secretly wish you could be like him.

Thank you, O God, for the temptation that comes to me through Jesus Christ. Help me to yield to it that I may find the joy which no one can take away. Amen.

MONDAY—Week 5

TEMPTED BY WHAT IS HIGH   Read Eccles. 12

They are afraid also of what is high.—Eccles. 12:5.

The author of Ecclesiastes gives a striking description of what happens when people begin to lose their youth. "They are afraid of that which is high." If a person sees a mountain and does not feel tempted to climb it and gain the view from the heights, he is getting old.

Anything unconquered is a challenge to the ambitious person. When men discovered it might be possible to land on the moon, they were not satisfied until they had done so. Now they are intrigued by the idea of exploring the heavenly bodies that are farther away.

Most people will never have a chance to be astronauts, but everyone has an opportunity to be an explorer in the moral and spiritual realm. Always there is the possibility of going farther.

Said James Ramsey Ullman, a member of the first party of Americans ever to reach the peak of Mt. Everest: "The response to challenge is the core and mainspring of man's nature. An ocean is there, cross it. A mountain is there, climb it. A challenge is there, meet it."

And one might add, "Jesus' life is there, match it."

38

Keep me from being satisfied with myself, O God. May I set my gaze on some high goal and put myself under the discipline that will enable me to attain it. Amen.

TUESDAY—Week 5

HOW HERCULES BECAME A HERO

Read Josh. 24:14-18

Choose this day whom you will serve.—Josh. 24:15

Hercules, according to the Greek legend, left his home in Thebes and started out to make his fortune. Soon he came to a fork in the road. In one direction the way was broad and pleasant with a downward slope. The other road was narrow and went gradually upward.

While he stood in doubt about which way to go, two young women came up and each offered to be his guide. One, who was gaily dressed, said, "Come with me, O Hercules, and I will take you over an easy path. You will never know hardship or pain." "What is your name?" asked Hercules. And the damsel replied, "Pleasure."

The other maiden quietly said, "I will not deceive you. Know that the gods give nothing without labor and effort. Come with me and I will make you strong." Hercules asked her name and she answered, "People call me Duty." Hercules stood for a moment in thought, then turned to Duty and said, "You shall be my guide." Then he followed her on the upward way that made him the hero of his people.

Always there is a high way and a low. And every person must decide which way his soul shall go.

Eternal God, you have placed me in a world where nothing worthwhile can be achieved without courage.

Give me the wisdom to make the right choice and to travel the high way. Amen.

WEDNESDAY—Week 5

CHOOSING THE MOUNTAIN   Read Josh. 14:6-15

Give me this mountain.—Josh. 14:12 (KJV)

When the children of Israel came into the promised land and the territory was divided, Caleb was given his choice. He was the oldest member of the conquering group and the person who, except for Joshua, had rendered the most faithful service.

Caleb was eighty-five years of age, but he was not afraid of a hard task. He might have been expected to select the fertile plains which would be easy to cultivate, but he pointed toward a mountain which was reputed to be occupied by giants. "Give me this mountain," he said. In spite of his age, he wanted to make his life count in the largest way. He chose the toughest job in the new land.

The Bible tells us nothing further about Caleb, but it is evident that the mountain was cleared from its enemies and its slopes transformed into meadows and orchards. Years later, David chose it as the capital of Israel and reigned there seven years before winning his way into Jerusalem.

Which do you choose: the mountain or the plain? An easy and comfortable existence with no problems to be solved and no battles to be fought? Or a life with creative possibilities, which will leave the world better than you found it?

Make me discontented, O God, with the life of the lowlands. Help me to keep looking upward. May I struggle toward an ever higher goal. Amen.

40

THURSDAY—Week 5

THE MAN WHO DIED CLIMBING   Read Ps. 61

Lead thou me to the rock that is higher than I.
—Ps. 61:2

Over the grave of an Alpine guide who lost his life on the mountainside is this inscription, "He died climbing." The words suggest what ought to be the attitude of every Christian. Always he should be trying to reach a higher goal.

Many people with a casual acquaintance with Christ join the church and become routine members. They seem to assume that they have reached the goal of the Christian life and no longer need to be striving upward. Not so with the person who is in earnest! He never reaches the place where he says, "At last I have arrived." He knows there is a still higher level to which he ought to aspire.

Jesus told his disciples that they should *strive* to enter the narrow gate. Note the literal meaning of the word in Greek. It is *agonize*. It suggests that we are to put forth an agony of effort, using every last ounce of determination and strength in responding to the upward call.

What a challenge it is to look up and see Christ beckoning to us and saying, "Come up higher. I am your guide and will give you the help that you need." Only a weakling will fail to respond.

May the time never come, O God, when I am ready to stop climbing. Each morning may I renew my vision of the goal and go forward with Christ as my guide. Amen.

LIFTED BY THE POWER OF GOD   Read Ps. 121

I will lift up my eyes to the hills. From whence does my help come? My help comes from the Lord.—Ps. 121: 1-2

If you have ever been on a boat as it went through a canal lock, you will understand what it means to be lifted by a power not your own. When the boat enters the lock, it is confronted by a concrete wall. If it must rely on its own strength, it can go no farther. While the boat quietly waits, the man in control of the lock closes the gate behind it. He then pushes a button and water rushes in from above. The vessel is lifted to a higher level and is free to continue its journey.

Christians often reach the limit of what they can accomplish by themselves. We seem hemmed in by our weakness and inadequate abilities, or by the circumstances surrounding us. We have made so little progress that we are discouraged and ready to give up. There may be a habit we cannot break, a temptation we are not strong enough to resist, a discouragement that keeps us moping in our room, a sorrow that leaves us in loneliness. How can we hope to go ahead?

Let God into your life. Link yourself to the spiritual power of the universe and the blank wall will soon disappear.

Dear God, lead me into a deeper understanding of the spiritual laws of the universe. Make me humble enough to accept the help which you are always ready to give. Amen.

SATURDAY—Week 5

TEMPTING OTHERS TO GOODNESS

Read Acts 5:12-16

Let your light so shine before men, that they may see your good works and give glory to your Father who is in heaven.—Matt. 5:16

The life of every person, through its unconscious influence, can be a temptation to better living. Like Peter, your shadow can have a healing effect wherever it falls.

Sir Walter Scott became involved in a staggering debt due to the bankruptcy of a publishing house in which he was an inactive partner. He might have compromised with the creditors but regarded the entire debt as personal. "If I live and retain my health," he said, "no man shall lose a penny by me." He started writing more intensively. Day after day, night after night, he gave himself to the task.

One evening a group of young men came together in a room in London to spend the night in drinking and gambling. Through the window across the street they saw Sir Walter Scott, old and ill, bent over his desk. The party broke up and the young men went home. They could not gamble their money as they thought of Scott's integrity and scrupulous honesty.

Owen Meredith said that no life
Can be pure in its purpose or strong in its strife
And all life not be purer and stronger thereby.

O God, keep me aware of the contagion of goodness. May I realize that it spreads not only by direct contact but even by the shadow which one life casts on another. May my life be a healing influence. Amen.

43

HOW TO FIND LIFE

THE QUESTION YOUTH IS ALWAYS ASKING
Read Mark 10:17-22

What must I do to inherit eternal life?—Mark 10:17

A young man stood on the window ledge of a New York skyscraper threatening to commit suicide. Several people, coming into the room behind the window, pleaded with him not to jump. Again and again he said, "I wish someone would convince me that life is worth living." Evidently no one gave him a satisfying answer, for he finally plunged to his death.

An amazing number of people have difficulty in finding meaning in life. An old book of conundrums has as its last question, "What is the greatest riddle of all?" The answer is, "The greatest riddle is life, for we must all give it up."

If you are seriously seeking to find out what life means, read the story of the rich young ruler. He went to Jesus with the question, "What must I do to inherit eternal life?" He was not asking how to get to heaven, for the word "eternal" deals with the quality of life as well as its duration. He wanted life so satisfying that one could enjoy living that way now and forever.

That is what we all want. Jesus stands before us and says, "I am the way."

Dear Heavenly Father, as I stand on the edge of life, I need thy guidance and help. Grant that I may not miss the happiness which I seek. Amen.

MONDAY—Week 6

RESPECT THE INSIGHTS OF THE PAST
Read Ex. 20:1-17

If you would enter life, keep the commandments.
—Matt. 19:17

Jesus' first suggestion to the rich young ruler was that he should keep the commandments. This is commonplace advice, but it is the beginning of all satisfying living. The ten commandments represent the great moral insights that have stood the test of human experience throughout thousands of years.

Respect the wisdom of the past. You will not find happiness by rebelling against it. We do not outgrow the past. We grow out of it. The great scientific discoveries of the modern world have been possible only because people have used the accumulated knowledge of previous generations and have built upon it.

Do not fool yourself into thinking it is otherwise in the moral and spiritual realm. We show our ignorance, and not our wisdom, if we think we can find life by lightly discarding what has been learned by previous seekers after the truth. A person may get a temporary thrill out of being a moral rebel, but after all the commandments have been broken, life can be as dull as it was before and even more unbearable.

Jesus refused to be bound by the past, but he built upon the moral foundations which had been laid by previous generations.

Make me humble, O God, as I think of my indebtedness to the great souls of the past. Teach me to cherish my heritage while I seek to make new discoveries of the truth. Amen.

TUESDAY—Week 6

NEGATIVE GOODNESS NOT ENOUGH
Read Matt. 19:23-30

All these I have observed; what do I still lack?
—Matt. 19:20

Although the rich young ruler had kept the commandments, he still had a haunting feeling that his life was empty. He had missed the thrill of great living. "What do I still lack?" he asked.

The reason he felt his life was not all it ought to be was that his goodness was negative. To refrain from breaking the law is not enough. He had done nothing bad, but had made no attempt to scale the heights of moral achievement. Although he was a man of wealth, he had made no personal sacrifice for the sake of helping people in need. Passive goodness is never enough, as Marguerite Wilkinson makes plain in her poem "Guilty":

> I never cut my neighbor's throat,
>   My neighbor's gold I never stole;
> I never spoiled his house and land,
>   But God have mercy on my soul!
> For I am haunted night and day
>   By all the deeds I have not done;
> O unattempted loveliness!
>   O costly valor never won!

46

Dear God, make me dissatisfied with the littleness of my life when it is centered in myself. Mold me into the kind of person whom you can use in the work of your kingdom. Amen.

WEDNESDAY—Week 6

AN ADVENTURE OF LOVE   Read Luke 16:19-31

If you would be perfect, go, sell what you possess and give to the poor.—Matt. 19:21

Jesus told the rich young ruler that he must respect the heritage of the past. Then he went on to say that a conventional morality, based on a traditional faith, is not enough to bring the thrill of great living. To be good in a dull, routine sort of way is perilously near to being good for nothing.

Seeking to jolt the man free from his self-centered complacency, Jesus challenged him to sell his possessions and give the money to the poor. Obviously Jesus did not intend this to be a binding command on all people, for he told Zaccheus that salvation had come to his house when the tax-gatherer promised to give half of his goods to feed the poor. Back of Jesus' words, however, is a great principle capable of universal application. One can never find great living on any cheap and easy basis. It involves sacrificial love, which is willing to pay the price of a costly identification with the needs of others.

For the Christian, the pot of gold containing the true riches of life is not to be found at the end of some daintily colored rainbow but at the foot of the cross.

O God, help me to make my life a glad adventure of love. Save me from being hemmed in by selfishness. Make me willing to be a brother to all mankind. Amen.

THE NECESSITY OF DECISION   Read Matt. 9:9-13

Commit your way to the Lord.—Ps. 37:5

Jesus ended his conversation with the rich young ruler by inviting him to be one of his disciples. He called for decision and dedication. Until one is willing to make a great commitment, he cannot discover the ultimate secret of great living.

A Christian is more than a decent person who leads a good life and performs a daily good turn. He accepts Christ as a revelation of the truth about life and commits himself to doing the will of God as it has been made known through Christ. A Christian must give himself to Christ as his Lord.

There are many times in life when it is difficult to make decisions, but what is most needed is one major commitment which sets a standard for all that you do. If you have come face to face with Christ and have been challenged by his life and teachings, it ought to be possible to see in him the highest and best that you know.

We do not need to wait until we have more knowledge about Christ or about life. The question is whether we will act on the knowledge we have.

O God, I hear the voice of Christ calling me to be his disciple. Help me to respond to his invitation and make the great Christian affirmation, Jesus Christ is my Lord. Amen.

FRIDAY—Week 6

A HAPPY LIFE CANNOT BE BOUGHT

Read Mark 10:23-31

How hard it will be for those who have riches to enter the kingdom of God!—Mark 10:23

After the rich young ruler had gone away, Jesus told his disciples that it would be hard for those who have riches to find life's highest satisfactions. The disciples were amazed. It was a common belief then, as now, that wealth is a sure source of happiness.

One of the basic truths of human experience is that happiness cannot be bought. Cecil Rhodes, who founded an empire in Africa and became one of England's richest men, was once asked if he was happy. "Good God, no," was his answer. He went on to express his admiration for General William Booth who, out of deep religious convictions, founded the Salvation Army and gave his life to the poor. Rhodes said he would give all he had for a life like that of Booth.

More recently, a reporter talked to a man who is perhaps the richest man of the United States, who admitted that he was not happy. He had been married and divorced five times and estranged from his children. He said, "I would give all I have for one happy marriage."

Do you want a satisfying life? Read again the story of the rich young ruler and meditate on its meaning for today.

O God, as I start out in life, give me the wisdom to choose the right road. May I not be misled by appearances or by the glamour of cheap joys. Amen.

SATURDAY—Week 6

THE GREAT REFUSAL   Read Matt. 26:20-25

He went away sorrowful.—Matt. 19:22

The rich young ruler refused the invitation to

be Jesus' follower. For him, money and position were all important. He loved himself so much that he could not reach out to include others in his love. Think of all he missed—an enriching companionship with Jesus, an opportunity for spiritual growth, a chance to be part of the immortal fellowship that constituted the first Christian church.

He missed the best because he was clinging to something less than the best. He kept the commandments, but he could not bring himself to accept the law of love. He refused to become the kind of man that, with Christ's help, he might have become. And we are all in danger of the same failure. Whittier's words, which may have been prompted by the story of the rich young ruler, could be a true description of our own destiny:

> O doom beyond the saddest guess,
> As the long years of God unroll,
> To make thy dreary selfishness
> The prison of a soul.

Set me free, O God, to be my best self. Help me to find the larger life which comes to those who lose themselves in their love for you and their fellowmen. Amen.

THE POWER TO BECOME

ARE YOU SATISFIED WITH YOURSELF?

Read 2 Tim. 3

For men will be lovers of self . . . rather than lovers of God, holding the form of religion but denying the power of it.—2 Tim. 3:2, 5.

The poet Shelley is said to have told about a dream in which a hooded figure appeared and beckoned him to follow. When the poet caught up with the apparition, he pulled the mask from its face and behold, the likeness was that of his own countenance. As Shelley gazed silently at this resemblance to himself, the figure asked, "Are you satisfied?"

This is a personal question every Christian needs to answer. Am I satisfied with my moral and spiritual attainments and my relationships with other people? But along with it goes a sterner question, "Is God satisfied with me?"

Even though we read the Bible occasionally and spend a few minutes in prayer, we often neglect to face the deeper meaning of the Christian life. We do what someone called "fooling ourselves with trivial devotions." We go through the forms of godliness but fail to lay hold on its power because we

51

do not make all life an offering to God. What we need is the moral and spiritual transformation which comes into our lives when we say with the Psalmist, "Lo, I come to do thy will, O God."

Keep me, O God, from being satisfied with my life as it is. Give me a deeper desire to find your purpose for my life and make me willing to follow your guidance. In Jesus' name. Amen.

MONDAY—Week 7

THE PERSON YOU MIGHT BE   Read Gal. 2:11-21

It is no longer I who live, but Christ who lives in me.—Gal. 2:20

An Italian play opens with a group of actors who are starting to rehearse a new drama. They are interrupted by a group of six characters who insist on being included in the presentation. They say they are in search of an author who can bring them to life by making them part of an actual play. "We are most interesting characters, sir," one of them said, "side-tracked, however." The stage manager asks them exactly what they want and they reply, "We want to live in you."

In the back of the imagination of the Italian author is a gripping truth. To every person on the stage of human experience there comes the possibility of a new and different self saying, "I want to live in you." Knocking again and again at the door of your heart is the person you might be, the capacities you might develop, the ideals you might realize. They plead to be allowed to express themselves in your life.

Oliver Wendell Holmes spoke of the people who

"die with all their music in them." The possible self is never realized because the person fails to lay hold on the inner power which would enable him to fulfill his possibilities.

Forgive me, O God, for failing to open the door of my heart more fully to the incoming of thy spirit. Help me to know what it means to have Christ live in me. Amen.

TUESDAY—Week 7

CHANGED BY CHRIST   Read John 1:35-43

Thou art Simon the son of Jona: thou shalt be called Cephas, which is by interpretation, a stone.—John 1:42 (KJV)

Nothing in all history is more striking than the change wrought in the lives of men by the influence of Christ. Peter, the vacillating fisherman, was transformed into a rock and became the cornerstone of the early Christian church. John, who was called Boanerges, or "the son of thunder," because of his fiery temper, became the disciple of love. Thomas the doubter was changed into a person of steadfast faith who is reputed to have carried the gospel to India. The hardened thief on the cross became the penitent sinner worthy of paradise. Paul, the persecutor of the early Christians, through a vision of Christ received the power to become the great apostle and saint.

Not only in the first century but through all subsequent generations, Christ has come to people and given them a victorious spirit. Perhaps in your own heart is a secret longing for a higher life. You may have made good resolutions and broken them so many times that you have almost given up trying.

Instead of relying on your own strength, bring into your life the new power which Christ stands ready to give.

O God, I am not strong enough to be what I want to be. Teach me what it means to rely on you with a trust that is full and complete. For Christ's sake. Amen.

WEDNESDAY—Week 7

THE PERSON GOD INTENDED   Read Luke 19:1-10

If any one is in Christ, he is a new creation. —2 Cor. 5:17

Lloyd Douglas in his novel *The Robe* has given a striking account of the influence of Jesus on Zaccheus. The Jericho tax gatherer felt highly honored to have Jesus go home with him to dinner, but he was uncomfortable in the presence of his guest. Aware of his own unworthiness, he avoided the Master's gaze. At last he gathered the courage to look directly into the eyes of Jesus and had difficulty in turning away. He arose and went to the door where a crowd of people had gathered in the hope of catching another glimpse of the famous visitor. Zaccheus announced to the amazed group, "I have resolved to give half of my goods to feed the poor. And if I have defrauded any man, I will make restitution."

When Zaccheus went back into the room, Jesus asked what caused him to take such a step. "Good Master," replied the tax collector, "I saw mirrored in your eyes the face of the Zaccheus I was meant to be."

Turn to the New Testament and read the Gospels thoughtfully. In the life of Jesus you will see a reflection of the person God intends us all to be. Keep looking at him and your life will become different.

Dear Father, give me a deeper insight into the things of the spirit. May I see Christ so clearly that I will never be able to turn away from him. Amen.

THURSDAY—Week 7

THE MAN WHO SAID GOOD-BYE TO GOD
Read John 5:39-47

**You refuse to come to me that you may have life.
—John 5:40**

Aaron Burr is one of the tragic figures in American history. Although he came from a distinguished family and was one of the brightest men ever to graduate from Princeton, his long life was neither useful nor happy.

It is a Princeton legend that when a series of religious meetings was being held on the campus, Burr shut himself in his room saying he intended to decide about his relationship to God. Late that night, the students in the adjoining room heard him throw open the shutters and exclaim, "Good-bye, God." Whether or not the story is actual fact, it is true that he made a god out of his own ambition.

He desperately wanted to be President and developed a bitter hatred of Alexander Hamilton, who opposed his nomination. Eventually Burr killed Hamilton in a duel and for the rest of his life was a lonely and forlorn individual.

Nathaniel Hawthorne left in his notebook a suggestion for a story "in which the principal character never appears." Although he never carried out the idea, the story has been written in countless lives because people lack the power to fulfill their possibilities.

O God of love and power, in my weakness may I lay hold on thy strength, that I may become the person you intended me to be. For Christ's sake. Amen.

FRIDAY—Week 7

LETTING GOD CONTROL YOUR LIFE

Read Phil. 4:8-13

I can do all things in him who strengthens me. —Phil. 4:13

A minister once used Kipling's poem "If" as the climax of a sermon to young people. He recited all the "ifs" which conclude with the idea that if you can do all these things, "You'll be a man, my son." As he finished, a youth in the back seat called out, "What if you can't?"

This is the question which has been asked repeatedly by those in the grip of evil habits. They have yielded to temptation so often that their will-power seems to be gone.

"What if you can't?" That question has been answered by thousands of people who were slaves of alcohol and were unable to break away from their bondage until they joined Alcoholics Anonymous. The first principle of the organization is that a person must admit his inability to manage his own life and say that he is willing to turn it over to the control of God. Those who have done this have had their lives made new.

It is not piosity to talk about letting God manage your life. The members of Alcoholics Anonymous have tried it and found that it works, when members band together to seek God's help.

56

Make me willing to confess my weakness, dear God, and to place my life under your management. Lead me into the new life for which I long. Amen.

SATURDAY—Week 7

TRANSFORMED INTO HIS LIKENESS

Read 2 Cor. 3:7-18

We all, with unveiled face, beholding the glory of the Lord, are being changed into his likeness.—2 Cor. 3:18

An old story tells about a prince who was tormented with self-pity because of his crooked back. When he gazed into the mirror he would try to imagine how he would appear if he had a straight body. One day he engaged a sculptor to make a statue of him without his deformity.

The sculptor carried out his commission to the satisfaction of the prince. The statue was then set up in a secluded corner of the palace garden. Every day the prince quietly followed the path that led to the statue. Looking at himself as he would be if he had a perfectly formed body, he instinctively threw back his shoulders and tried to stand erect. Months later he went to the royal tailor to be measured for a new suit. Taking out his tape, the tailor looked at the prince in surprise. "Something has happened," he said, "you are a different man."

Take time each day to look at the Christ who represents what man at his best can be, and you will begin to be transformed into his likeness. You do not change yourself. You are changed by "beholding the glory of the Lord."

Each day, dear God, may I go to some quiet place where I can gaze on the face of Christ. By looking at him may I become like him. For his sake. Amen.

57

A BOOK FOR YOUTH

SUNDAY—Week 8

DISCOVERING THE BIBLE　　Read 2 Kings 22:1-10

I have found the book.—2 Kings 22:8

A fifteen-year-old boy from Bethlehem by the name of Muhammad the Wolf was looking for strayed goats from his father's flock, which was grazing along the north shore of the Dead Sea. In his search he came near some caves in the cliffs above. He threw a stone into the entrance hoping it would drive out the goats if they happened to be there.

What he heard was not the bleating of goats but the sound of breaking pottery. Making a difficult climb to get to the cave, he found a number of big jars containing leather scrolls. They turned out to be the most valuable collection of ancient manuscripts discovered in modern times. One was a scroll of Isaiah which goes back to the first century before Christ and is the oldest existing biblical manuscript. The scrolls were the work of a monastic group known as Essenes in the Qumram colony.

The boy made his discovery by chance. It will not be by accident, however, that young people will make their own discovery of the Bible. Thoughtful

and intelligent reading is necessary. The results
will be found to be worth the effort.

**Forgive me, dear Father, that I have paid so little
attention to the Bible. May I no longer leave my reading
to chance, but develop some plan which will help me to
discover its value for my life. Amen.**

MONDAY—Week 8

THE BIBLE BELONGS TO YOUTH

Read 1 John 2:7-17

I write to you, young men, because you are strong.
—1 John 2:14

The Bible is a book which young people can rightly claim as their own. No one need think that its
message is for the old or those about to die. It shows
how to live. Its main character was a dynamic young
carpenter who did all his work before he was thirty-
three years old. He lived long enough, however, to
discover the secret of happiness and to start a
youth movement that changed the course of history.

The people who were Jesus' intimate friends and
most constant companions were also young. Probably they were not as old as he. The first century
in Palestine was a time and place when people
married young, and Peter seems to have been the
only one who had a wife. In Jesus' last conversation
with the disciples he addressed them as "children."
One reason his followers were able to exert such a
tremendous influence on the future of mankind was
that they had the enthusiasm of youth.

Let no teenager assume that the Bible is not for
him. It tells how young people can live in a changing
world and have a happy and victorious experience.

O God, teach me how to live. Make me willing to learn from Jesus and put into my heart the faith and daring of the kingdom of God. In Jesus' name. Amen.

TUESDAY—Week 8

FOOD THAT LEAVES A SWEET TASTE

Read Ezek. 3:1-11

Then I ate it; and it was in my mouth as sweet as honey.—Ezek. 3:3

When Ezekiel was called to be a prophet to the Jewish people in exile in Babylon, he had a unique vision. An angel held before him a scroll which contained the Law of the Lord and commanded him to eat it. When he opened his mouth and tasted it, he found that it was as sweet as honey. This seemed to be a surprise to him. Evidently he expected the commands of the Lord to have a bitter taste.

The Bible is a book to be devoured. We are not to peruse it in a casual way, but to eat it, digest it, assimilate its truth, and make it a part of our inner selves. When we do this, we will find that it is not only spiritually nourishing, but sweet and satisfying. God's purpose for us is not to make us miserable but to help us to be happy.

The Bible calls us to a life of integrity and love. It insists that we must love God and our fellowmen, go the second mile, and do more than our duty. We may be afraid these principles will make life bitter. Not so! They will bring lasting inner satisfaction.

Dear Father, give me the faith that thy purpose for my life is wiser and better than any that I could form for myself. May I gladly seek thy will and do it. Amen.

THE CENTRAL FIGURE OF THE BIBLE
Read John 7:10-17

These are written that you may believe that Jesus is the Christ, the Son of God, and that believing you may have life in his name.—John 20:31

Mark Twain began his famous novel *Huckleberry Finn* by saying, "You wouldn't know me without you have read a book called *The Adventures of Tom Sawyer*." The sentence is not grammatical, but it immediately acquaints the reader with the main character of the story.

Similar words could be used about the central figure in the story of Christianity. You probably wouldn't know about Christ unless you had first read the Bible. The Old Testament gives us a history of the Jewish people and of the background from which Jesus came. The New Testament contains the record of his life and teachings and the story of the early church.

Many people seem to assume that they can be good followers of Christ without paying much attention to the Scriptures. They read passages here and there, but never take time to become familiar with the whole story. A woman, describing how she read a magazine, said, "I just skim through it, like the Bible." Skimming is not enough. You can never be a real Christian without thoughtful study of the Scriptures and a willingness to open your mind to their truth.

Strengthen my desire, dear God, to know more about Jesus Christ. Make me more willing to give time and thought to the study of the Bible that the thoughts of Christ may become my thoughts. In his name. Amen.

THURSDAY—Week 8

THE SOURCE OF LIBERTY   Read Luke 15:1-10

You will know the truth and the truth will make you free.—John 8:32

Do you know the origin of the famous phrase used by Lincoln in his Gettysburg address about government "of, by, and for" the people? It is in the preface of John Wycliffe's translation of the Bible into the English language in 1382. He said: "The Bible is for the government of the people, by the people, and for the people."

The stream of liberty which started flowing through America with the earliest settlers, and still showers us with its blessings, had its origin in the Scriptures. For a hundred years in colonial America, the Bible was the book from which people learned to read. All intelligent people became familiar with its great truth about the sacredness of the individual in the sight of God. Instilled in the minds of those who signed the Declaration of Independence was the idea that liberty was one of the "inalienable rights" which came from the Creator. No dictator had a right to enslave a person, because man belonged to God.

Are you concerned about the future of government by the people? Then you can do nothing more practical than study and teach the Bible, which is the source of mankind's great liberating ideas.

God of our fathers, whose devotion to the truths of the Bible achieved our liberty, grant that we may remain a strong and great people because of our obedience to thy Word. Amen.

FRIDAY—Week 8

THE BIBLE CAN MAKE YOU RICH

Read Matt. 13:44-51

The ordinances of the Lord are true and righteous altogether. More to be desired are they than gold.
—Ps. 19:9-10

When a young man went to college, his mother bought a new Bible and packed it with his clothes and other belongings. Not until his senior year did he find the ten dollar bill which she had placed between the pages at the beginning of the New Testament. Many times he had been short of money and could have used some extra cash. Because he neglected the Bible, he was poorer than he needed to be.

Is this not a parable of what happens when we go week after week without opening our Bibles? We remain spiritually poor. We fail to receive the stimulus of great ideas which will enrich our minds and feed our spirits. If we are not familiar with the Psalms, we have missed one of the greatest expressions of religious joy. If we have not read the Gospels, we have overlooked the story of the greatest life the world has ever known. If we have not read the thirteenth chapter of First Corinthians, we have neglected one of literature's greatest poems on love.

Get out your Bible. It is a storehouse of spiritual treasure. Why skimp along in spiritual poverty when the Bible can make you rich?

Grant, O God, that my life may be enriched by finding the treasure contained in the Bible. Teach me how to study and use it so that I may have its full value for my life. In Jesus' name. Amen.

SATURDAY—Week 8

A BOOK TO BE FOLLOWED   Read Eph. 6:10-20

Take the helmet of salvation, and the sword of the Spirit, which is the Word of God.—Eph. 6:17

A boy who died when he was only sixteen years of age is said to have started a custom which has been followed for four centuries in crowning a British king. After the coronation of Edward VI in Westminster Abbey, a great procession started for the banquet hall.

In front of the youthful ruler were three soldiers carrying swords. When he asked what they stood for, he was told that they represented the three united countries of England, Scotland, and Wales. "There is one more sword which should be with them," said Edward who had been well schooled in the Scriptures and tried to guide his life by them. He added, "It is the Bible, which is the sword of the Spirit." At his suggestion, the pulpit Bible was brought from the Abbey and placed at the head of the parade. At every coronation since that time the Bible has been presented to the monarch with the words "This is the most valuable thing this world affords."

As you start out in life, put the Bible at the head of your procession. And all through your earthly pilgrimage use your influence to give the Bible a more exalted place in the affairs of your community and nation.

I thank you for the Bible, O God. Grant that for me it may be not only a book to be admired and praised, but one which I keep before me as a daily guide. Amen.

64

A RELIGION OF MY OWN

THE GOSPEL ACCORDING TO ME Read Rom. 2:1-16

According to my gospel.—Rom. 2:16

The first four books of the New Testament all tell the good news about Jesus' life and death and resurrection. Each one, however, is written from a different viewpoint, depending on the author's personal interest and interpretation.

Matthew was especially concerned with the teachings of Jesus and gives us the Sermon on the Mount. Mark includes less of Jesus' teaching than the other Gospels, but was deeply impressed by what Jesus did as a man of action. Luke was a Gentile and a doctor and his book reflects his background. The last of the four gospels was written by John at a time when Christianity was coming into intimate contact with Greek thought. He interpreted Christianity in a way that would make its meaning clear to those brought up in a Grecian culture.

Before any of the other writings came the letters of the apostle Paul. He tells about his own personal vision and how it transformed his life. He thought of the gospel as especially his own and said, "According to my gospel." The challenge for each Christian is to have a religion which comes out of his own study of the Bible and his own experience with Christ.

Dear Father, I pray that I may be led into a deeper experience with Christ. May I have a religion which is my own because I have lived by it, tested its truth, and am willing to recommend it to others. Amen.

MONDAY—Week 9
MAKING RELIGION AN INNER EXPERIENCE
Read Ps. 34

O taste and see that the Lord is good!—Ps. 34:8

The Psalmist urged his friends to *taste* religion, that they might learn that God is good. Notice that there is a great difference between taste and the other four senses: hearing, sight, smell, and touch. Think of your own experience in eating a good dinner. You hear your mother say that the meal is ready. As you enter the dining room, you begin to smell the food. Then you see it on the table. As the dishes are passed, you touch them and know that they are hot. The food does you no good, however, until you taste it and allow it to become part of yourself.

So it is with religion. Someone can tell you how good it is. You can get a whiff of it by going to church or associating with religious people. You can touch it by picking up a Bible with its record of Jesus' life and teachings. But not until you actually taste religion, and take it into your inner self, does it begin to satisfy your spiritual hunger.

If religion is to do us any good, we must have one which is really our own.

66

Forgive me, O God, that my religion is so superficial. Lead me into a deeper understanding of its truth. May I have the experience of the Psalmist, who entrusted his life to your keeping and became sure of your goodness. Amen.

TUESDAY—Week 9

THE DISEASE OF ECHOLALIA   Read John 4:27-42

It is no longer because of your words that we believe, for we have heard for ourselves, and know that this is indeed the Savior of the world.—John 4:42

In the disease called "echolalia," the person repeats involuntarily everything that is said in his presence. Without realizing what he is doing, he imitates every conversation that he overhears.

Many people who call themselves Christian have a similar affliction. They live in a cave of religious echoes. Instead of doing any independent thinking, they repeat what they have heard other persons say. They have never wrestled with the problems of what a thoughtful person can honestly believe.

Some things in life can be borrowed. Your friend can loan you an umbrella or a raincoat; but religion, if it is to have any vital meaning, must come out of your own firsthand experience with God. Your friend can help you understand the Bible and stimulate your interest, but only when you make a personal decision to be a follower of Jesus Christ does religion begin to be a power in your life.

A traditional faith, handed down from the past and taught by one's parents or a Sunday school teacher, is better than none, but no intelligent young person ought to be satisfied to echo the faith of others. He needs to be able to say with Paul, "I know whom I have believed."

O God, keep me from being satisfied with a half-truth or from clinging to some pious error. Give me a faith that comes out of my own thinking and my own experience with thee. Amen.

WEDNESDAY—Week 9

LOVING GOD WITH YOUR MIND   Read Matt. 22:34-40

You shall love the Lord your God with all your heart, and with all your soul, and with all your mind. —Matt 22:37

The people who are critical of the Christian faith are often those who know the least about it. They have never given it any deep thought and have no real knowledge of what it means. Actually they have no adequate experience on which to base their judgment. Such was the case with Edmund Halley, the astronomer after whom Halley's comet is named. He was so outspoken in his atheism that Sir Isaac Newton, the greatest scientist of his day, gave him a stinging rebuke.

Said Newton, "I always attend to you, Dr. Halley, with the greatest deference when you do us the honor to converse on astronomy or mathematics, because they are subjects which you have industriously investigated and well understand. But religion is a subject on which I always hear you with pain, because this is a subject which you have not seriously examined and do not comprehend. You despise it because you have not studied it, and you will not study it because you despise it."

If the scoffer would give thoughtful study to the life and teachings of Jesus and pattern his own life after them, even for a brief time, his scorn might turn to praise.

Make me willing, O God, to pay the price of an intelligent faith which is based on deep conviction. Then may I give it the loyalty of my life. Amen.

THURSDAY—Week 9

THE DAY THAT CHANGED A LIFE

Read 2 Tim. 1:8-14

I am not ashamed, for I know whom I have believed. —2 Tim. 1:12

A magazine article describes "The Day that Changed My Life." It is a true story of a young woman who became so different that her influence changed the atmosphere of the office in which she worked. Her employer wanted to know what had happened to her.

She told him that some months previously she had made up her mind to live for an entire day as if there were a God who really loves people and cares for them, and guides and judges them. She had heard occasional sermons about God, but on this particular day she had decided to live as though the Christian faith were absolutely true. It made such a difference in her work and relationships with other people that she continued the experiment a second day. She kept on for a week and then for three months. God had now become the greatest fact in her experience, and she decided that this was the way she wanted to live for the rest of her life.

She had been a Christian by hearsay. Now she was a Christian by her own choice and conviction because she found the experience so satisfying. Her experiment is worth trying.

Dear God, give me the courage to put my faith to

the test. May I have the experience of Job when he said, "I had heard of thee by the hearing of the ear, but now my eye sees thee." Amen.

FRIDAY—Week 9

PRACTICING OUR RELIGION   Read Luke 5:1-11

Put out into the deep and let down your nets for a catch.—Luke 5:4

A famous story by Kierkegaard, a Danish writer, tells how a flock of geese lived in a yard with a fence around it. One day a goose from far away flew over the fence and told them that no bird with wings ought to be satisfied to live in such cooped-up quarters. He spoke of the way other geese had used their wings to fly through the boundless spaces of the sky. And he reminded them of the goodness of their Creator, who had given them wings with which they could launch out on a flight to distant places.

The geese were pleased with the words of their visitor. They approved his remarks and commended him for having made them a visit. But there was one thing they failed to do. They did not try to use their wings. They continued to waddle around the barnyard and eat the food which they found there.

Many so-called Christians are like the geese who refused to fly. They enjoy reading about great Christians like Dr. Schweitzer in Africa and others who have trusted their lives to God in an adventure of love. But instead of spreading their wings, they go on living in the same old way.

Dear God, free me from my bondage to easy and aimless living. As I think about the life of Christ, help me to offer my life to the service of his kingdom and to launch out in some adventure of love. Amen.

MAKING CHRIST REAL TO OTHERS

Read Phil. 1:19-30

For to me to live is Christ.—Phil. 1:21

Years ago I had the privilege of attending the Oberammergau Passion Play. The part of Jesus was played by Alois Lang, a tall man with a robust physique who made Jesus appear to the audience as a stalwart figure with a commanding personality. His acting had the mark of sincerity. He identified himself so completely with the Christ he was portraying that for many years, in trying to visualize Jesus, I have thought of Alois Lang.

After the play was over, I called on Mr. Lang in the little wood-carving shop which adjoined his home. I told him how much I appreciated his interpretation of Jesus' character. He thanked me very modestly and said nothing could make him happier than to know that he helped make the life of the Master more real to some other person.

This is something we all can do in the drama of daily life. It is not enough to read the gospels and have a casual acquaintance with Jesus. We need to allow his spirit of love and helpfulness and righteous indignation to be expressed through our own personalities. To make Christ more real by trying to be like him, this is a way in which we can render a high spiritual service to those with whom we associate.

In all humility, O God, may I seek to reflect the spirit of Christ. Give me his long-suffering patience with other people, his indignation at wrong, and his forgetfulness of self in the service of others. Amen.

71

MY BODY IS A TEMPLE

SUNDAY—Week 10

THE BODY IS GOD'S DWELLING PLACE
Read Luke 2:1-14

In the beginning was the Word, and the Word was with God, and the Word was God. . . . And the Word became flesh and dwelt among us.—John 1:1, 14

When God wished to make himself more fully known to men, he entered into the body of a carpenter in Nazareth. This is called the Doctrine of the Incarnation. It is not easy to understand, but one aspect of its truth is that the body can be the dwelling place of the spirit of God. The Christian, therefore, seeks to serve God with his body as well as his soul.

It is significant that the words "holy" and "healthy" come from the same Anglo-Saxon word which means "whole." To be holy, then, one must guard his health and have his whole being dedicated to God. It is a sin to become ill through carelessness or neglect, for we can no longer do our best work for God.

The Christian is under a solemn obligation to use his body at all times as a trust from God. He seeks to make God the Lord of all life. To worship God is not only to bow in prayer, or to go to church and

72

join in singing his praise and listening to the reading of the Bible, but by making our daily lives, as we live them in our human bodies, an offering to God.

O God, give me a deeper reverence for my body. Grant that I may be able to keep myself physically fit and be ready for whatever you would have me do. Amen.

MONDAY—Week 10

THE PHYSICAL VITALITY OF JESUS
Read Matt. 21:12-17

The child grew and became strong.—Luke 2:40

The Bible tells us very little about the boyhood of Jesus, but what we do know indicates that he was sturdy and strong. When he was twelve years of age, he went on a long hike from Nazareth to Jerusalem to attend the Passover with his parents. The trip was ninety miles each way. When old enough to work, he followed the trade of Joseph, who was a carpenter. It was long before the time of labor-saving devices. Carpenters cut down their own trees and hewed the lumber into the desired shape. Jesus' muscles were hard and his shoulders strong from handling the ax and lifting heavy beams into place.

During the years of his public ministry, Jesus walked back and forth across Palestine for hundreds of miles. He hiked and rowed and climbed mountains and slept under the open sky. Only a rugged man could have stood that kind of living. He was such a dominant personality that no one opposed him when he drove the money changers out of the temple and overturned their tables.

73

One thing is sure. Jesus was no weakling. If one seriously becomes a follower of Jesus, he should make it his sacred duty to keep his body at its best.

Dear God, may the strength and vigor of Jesus' life be a standard for my own. Teach me that a neglected body is evidence that a person is not seriously trying to be a Christian. Amen.

TUESDAY—Week 10

PHYSICAL NEGLECT IS INGRATITUDE

Read Rom. 12:1-3

Present your bodies as a living sacrifice, holy and acceptable to God.—Rom. 12:1

From ancient Jewish literature comes a story about the great teacher, Hillel. He ended a long session with his disciples on a warm day by saying, "Now I am going to perform a religious duty." "What duty is it?" they asked. "That of taking a bath," replied Hillel. When his pupils seemed surprised at the answer, he added: "Ought I not to take care of my body? Was it not created in the likeness of God?"

If we neglect the body, we are failing to show our gratitude for one of God's greatest gifts. To be careless of one's health is to be indifferent to our spiritual obligations. If a person has a strong body, he ought to thank God and do his best to keep it in healthy condition. If his body is weak or diseased, he should use every possible means to bring it back to its highest state of efficiency.

Young people usually have good health. It is their religious duty to preserve it. Part of a Christian's responsibility is to keep himself clean, eat a balanced diet, get adequate sleep and exercise, and keep free from habits that may eventually undermine his physical well-being.

Forgive me, O God, if I have ignored the laws of health. May I show my love for you by keeping my body strong and well. Amen.

WEDNESDAY—Week 10

TEMPLE OR TAVERN?   Read 1 Cor. 6:12-20

Do you not know that your body is a temple of the Holy Spirit within you?—1 Cor. 6:19

"My body was a tavern, but now it is a temple." This is the way a man described the change that Christ made in his life. He had been an alcoholic, but found in Christ the power to free himself from the habits that formerly enslaved him. Once he despised his body because he could not control its appetites. Now he thought of it as a place worthy of the presence of God.

Tavern or temple! Think of the difference. One is a place for self-indulgence and the other a place for worship. A man goes to a tavern to forget his responsibilities. He enters a temple to renew his strength and courage and find the power to be a better man.

Napoleon, during his campaign in Germany, kept his horses in the Cologne cathedral. He was so completely lacking in reverence that he held nothing sacred. The building which was dedicated to God, and is one of the world's most famous places of worship, was turned into a stable for animals. Anyone with a sense of decency resents such desecration, but how often we forget that the body is a temple which belongs to God and should be kept fit for his use.

Dear Father, I thank you for this temple in which I have the privilege of living. Help me to keep it clean and ready at all times for your service. Amen.

THURSDAY—Week 10
RESPECTING THE BODILY TEMPLE

Read 1 Cor. 3:16-23

Glorify God in your body.—1 Cor. 6:20

One way to glorify God is by your physical appearance. Keep yourself neat and clean and well dressed. Since God has given us our bodies, we should seek to make them attractive.

Back in the middle ages, many people in Europe thought they were being religious when they paid no attention to their bodies. They withdrew into the desert, lived on as little food as possible, went without bathing, and allowed themselves to become dirty and ragged. They deluded themselves with the idea that they were being especially acceptable to God. Today you can still see so-called holy men in India who consider their dirty clothes and slovenly appearance as signs of their religious devotion. All this is in sharp contrast to the impression Jesus made on the people of his day. He was the kind of man whose coming brought rejoicing and hope.

There is something depressing about a temple which has been badly neglected. We feel instinctively that, if people really love God, they should take care of the building dedicated to his worship. Should not a Christian also be concerned about the bodily temple intended for the service of God?

O God, help me to live in such a way that my daily life will reflect thy glory and be a witness to my Christian faith. In Jesus' name. Amen.

OUR INFLUENCE ON OTHERS   Read Rom. 14:1-13

Decide never to put a stumbling-block or hindrance in the way of a brother.—Rom. 14:13

No one can use his body wrongly without hurting other people as well as himself. A mother urged her son to stop drinking. He brushed her off by saying, "I don't drink very much, and it is really my own business." A month later he smashed the family car, permanently injured his companion, and placed himself in the hospital. His family was involved in a heartbreaking experience.

People often defend premarital sex by saying, "It's all right so long as no one gets hurt." But again and again someone does get hurt. In spite of modern knowledge about the cure and prevention of venereal disease, the number of cases is a cause for deep concern. And can it be rightly said that no one is hurt because neither pregnancy nor disease results? The foundation for a happy and permanent home has been weakened. When each person knows that his partner once took an easygoing attitude toward sex, it is easy for suspicion to arise after marriage. Each is more apt to doubt the faithfulness of the other.

No one lives in complete isolation. Each life is so interwoven with others that everything we do has consequences in lives other than our own.

O God, I pray that I may never make it easy for others to do wrong. May I always remember that I am my brother's keeper. Amen.

STRENGTH OUT OF WEAKNESS   Read 2 Cor. 12:1-10

When I am weak, then I am strong.—2 Cor. 12:10

Physical fitness is one of life's greatest assets, yet many people have made amazing achievements in spite of disease and bodily limitations. By determination and skill they have surpassed those who were more favorably endowed. No one, whatever his handicap, should give up in despair and think that the doors of useful living are closed to him. Said Charles Darwin: "If I had not been so great an invalid, I would not have accomplished so much as I have."

The apostle Paul had a physical affliction which he called "a thorn in the flesh." Biblical scholars are not sure what is meant by the "thorn," but agree that it was a bodily impairment which made it difficult for him to do his best work.

Three times Paul prayed that the thorn might be removed. The answer to his prayer was not the removal of his problem but the words, "My grace is sufficient for thee." The affliction became a spur to seek God's help and make a greater effort. This finally enabled him to say, "When I am weak, then I am strong." In spite of his handicap he introduced Christianity into the Greek-speaking world and helped to change the course of history.

Dear Father, keep me from becoming discouraged. Whatever my difficulties, may I seek from you the strength that will make me faithful and courageous in spite of my weakness. Amen.

ON BEING UP-TO-DATE

KEEPING UP WITH CHANGE   Read Matt. 5:17-26

Unless your righteousness exceeds that of the scribes and Pharisees, you will never enter the kingdom of heaven.—Matt. 5:10

One of the greatest influences in modern life is the desire to keep up with the rapidly changing times. The eyes of mankind are directed toward the future. Everyone wants to be thought forward-looking and progressive. Advertising in the newspapers and over television constantly plays upon this theme. We are told that the latest model car is better because it has new features. Styles in clothing change every year. Men's neckties become wider or narrower. Women's skirts go up or down.

Changes are not important when they deal with externals, but they should have careful scrutiny when it comes to standards of right or wrong. We need to ask whether the proposed change is actually better. If we are to be really up-to-date, we must be able to discern the causes and ideas which will lead us forward into a better future.

In the Sermon on the Mount, Jesus urged people not to be bound by the past, but to see clearly the principles that create a firm foundation for better living. Jesus said he came not to destroy the teachings of the Old Testament but to fulfill them. He appealed to people to live by higher standards than those of previous generations.

O God, help me to understand that the old is not always false and that the new is not always true. May I find the truth as it has been made known by Christ. Amen.

MONDAY—Week 11

OLD BUT NOT OUTGROWN   Read Ps. 119:97-112

Thy word is a lamp to my feet and a light to my path.—Ps. 119:105

A New York City minister was in the office of a business executive who had a Bible on his desk. Everything else about the room was completely modern. The man thought he saw a look of surprise on the minister's face as he looked at the Bible. "That book is the most up-to-date thing in this plant," said the executive. "Equipment wears out and furnishing styles change, but this book is so far ahead of us that it can never be considered behind the times."

The man went on to tell how the Bible had been a creative influence in his life at a time when everything seemed to be going wrong. It had helped to change his thinking and had given him a new outlook on his problems. No book can be considered outdated if it can bring hope and help to a discouraged person.

There are two types of books: those that give information and those that bring inspiration. In a rapidly changing world, books of knowledge must frequently be rewritten. On the other hand, books of inspiration can have added value and authority because their ideas have been verified by the experience of people in all sorts of circumstances over centuries of time.

More than anything else, O God, I need the guidance and inspiration that will help me to lead a good life. Keep me from neglecting my Bible. Amen.

TUESDAY—Week 11

IS JESUS A BACK NUMBER?　　　Read Heb. 13:7-21

Jesus Christ is the same yesterday, today, and for ever.—Heb. 13:8

"Cheer up, Katie, Jesus is a back number." The quotation is from a letter written a generation ago by D. H. Lawrence, British playwright, to Katherine Mansfield, who was troubled by her lack of religious faith. The envelope enclosing the letter bore a date which was figured from the year Jesus was born. We can hardly consider him a back number when we still divide time into two eras, before Christ and after, and stamp our envelopes and newspapers from the time of his birth.

The fact that Jesus lived over 1900 years ago is no reason for thinking he does not have a vital meaning for our day. A distinguished psychiatrist, in speaking about the needs of the modern world, said we would have Utopia if we applied Jesus' teaching about loving our neighbor as ourselves. He added: "In fact, the hope of the world rests on our capacity to love, because it is the only way to neutralize the hate that comes from the deepest layers of our personalities." When it comes to love,

81

no one can say Jesus is out-of-date. He is so far ahead of us that we will have to hurry if we are to stand a chance of catching up with him.

Dear God, make us willing to go to Jesus to learn the meaning of love. Keep us from putting off the time when we begin to take his teaching seriously. In his name. Amen.

WEDNESDAY—Week 11

THE COURAGE TO BE MODERN   Read Prov. 23:29-35

They stagger with strong drink; they err in vision, they stumble in giving judgment.—Isa. 28:7.

Young people often think they are being really modern when they start to use liquor or drugs. Think a moment, however, and you will realize that such practices are a part of ancient history. Alexander the Great conquered the world, only to be defeated by his appetite for alcohol. When only thirty-three years of age, he died of an illness resulting from exposure after a drunken spree. Go farther back in history and read the Genesis story of Noah. After surviving the deluge in the ark, he had a chance to build a new world but one of the first things he did was to become disgustingly drunk.

The use of drugs for their exhilarating effect is also far from new. Opium smoking was a well-known habit in ancient China.

Do not fool yourself by thinking you are being sophisticated when you experiment with drinking and drugs. There is an attitude which is far more modern. It is to have the wisdom and courage to examine such practices from the long-range standpoint. Assess their social consequences and their

82

effect on personal health and happiness, and you will decide to leave them alone.

Heavenly Father, keep me from being deceived by old practices masquerading as modern and by evil disguised as good. May I never swerve from what in my own heart I believe to be right. Amen.

THURSDAY—Week 11

WHY BE OLD-FASHIONED ABOUT SEX?

Read Matt. 5:27-32

Get yourselves a new heart and a new spirit.—Ezek. 18:31

Many people are rebelling against ideas of morality which they consider old-fashioned. They insist on being free from the sex standards of the past. What they fail to realize is that they may be allowing themselves to be deceived by old customs dressed up in a new disguise.

A permissive attitude toward sex is hoary with age. Go back to the time of Heraclitus, one of the great thinkers of Greece who lived in Ephesus five hundred years before Christ. He is known in history as the weeping philosopher. No one could live in his city, he said, without being moved to tears by the immorality all around him. The temple of Artemis in Ephesus was listed as one of the seven wonders of the ancient world because of the beauty of its architecture. It served as a home for several hundred prostitutes, who were also considered to be priestesses. The Ephesians literally worshiped sex.

There is nothing new about premarital intercourse or promiscuous sex. What is far more modern is the idea of one man and one woman loving each other so much that they would not think of sexual intercourse until they had been united in the sacred bonds of marriage.

O God, give me reverence for my own personality and that of others. Help me to discipline my desires and give me wisdom to discern the true sources of enduring love and happiness. Amen.

FRIDAY—Week 11

IS CHRISTIANITY IRRELEVANT?   Read John 6:66-71

Lord, to whom shall we go? You have the words of eternal life.—John 6:68

A few years ago, John Lennon, one of the Beatles, said that Christianity has become irrelevant. "Christianity will go," he asserted. "It will vanish and shrink. We, the Beatles, are more popular than Jesus Christ."

How conceited he was! For most people, the Beatles will soon be only a vague memory, but it is a safe prediction that Jesus Christ will still be revered all over the world. The appeal of Jesus is not based on a passing popularity which comes from tickling the ear of the crowd but on his ability to help people understand the meaning of life and develop resources for satisfying living.

Jesus gives us our clearest and most satisfying picture of what God is like and of what man ought to become. "I am the light of the world," said Jesus. No one has done so much to illuminate our human existence. Emerson said that the name of Jesus "is not so much written as ploughed into the history of the world." He is the source of the finest aspects of our civilization.

84

Said Ernest Renan, the French philosopher, in words that might well be recalled by the Beatles, "Whatever the surprises of history, Jesus will not be surpassed."

O God, I thank you for Jesus Christ. When old things are passing away and the world seems to be in a turmoil, I turn to him as the solid rock on which I can base my life and look forward to the future with faith and hope. Amen.

SATURDAY—Week 11

DID CHRIST COME TOO SOON?   Read Gal. 4:1-11

When the time had fully come, God sent forth his Son. —Gal. 4:4

"He came too soon, this Christ," said the Malayan princess in Maxwell Anderson's play *The Wingless Victory*. She had saved the life of a Salem sea captain who married her and brought her back to live in his hometown. Although the princess accepted the Christian faith with simple sincerity, the friends of her husband remained bitterly prejudiced against her. She tried to win their friendship with kindness but was continually rebuffed.

At last she gave up in despair. Renouncing her Christian faith, she returned to the religion of her ancestors. She took her two children and a bottle of poison and headed for the ship to end her struggle. She said men were not yet ready for the Christ of peace. He had come too soon.

Did Christ come too soon? Is it not rather that we have failed to catch up with him? Paul said Jesus came in the fullness of time. The world needed him in the first century and it needs him now.

Modern means of transportation and communication have made all people neighbors, but they have not learned to live together in a world community. We need Jesus to teach us to love our neighbors as ourselves.

We thank thee, O God, for all the blessings that have come to our world through the life and teachings of Christ. Make us more worthy of being called his disciples. Amen.

THE CREATIVE USE OF LEISURE

SUNDAY—Week 12

THE NEW AGE OF LEISURE   Read John 10:1-10

I came that they may have life, and have it abundantly.—John 10:10

Back in the year 1516 a British statesman and scholar by the name of Sir Thomas More wrote a book called *Utopia*. It gave his vision of an ideal civilization which was established on an imaginary island. A major aspect of its perfect life was a shortened work week limited to sixty hours. From the standpoint of the reduced time required for labor, most Americans have been living in Utopia for many years. And there is no question but that in the future the number of workdays will grow fewer and shorter.

Will this result in having better citizens and a finer type of civilization? It remains to be seen. Increased leisure can be a blessing or a curse, depending on whether or not people learn to use their free time in creative ways.

Every year Americans spend billions of dollars trying to have a good time, but fail to succeed in their aim. Life has grown so increasingly empty and meaningless that the suicide rate has greatly increased, especially among young people. To learn to use time in a way that is personally enriching and socially helpful is one of the finest services that can now be rendered to society.

Dear Father, teach me how to live. Keep me from cheating myself and other people by frittering away my time on things that have no value. In Jesus' name. Amen.

MONDAY—Week 12

GOD'S GIFT OF TIME   Read Gen. 1:1-5

This is the day which the Lord has made; let us rejoice and be glad in it.—Ps. 118:24

One of the first acts of God, according to the Genesis story, was to divide light from darkness and create day. Time, then, belongs to God. He entrusts it to us as one of his greatest blessings that it may be a source of joy and gladness, but we must remember that we are stewards and not owners.

"I have no time," we often hear people say. "I have no time, even for myself." For a Christian, this is literal truth. His hours are rightly used only under the direction of God.

Although time is a gift of God, the days of the week are named after pagan deities. Sunday was named after the sun and Monday after the moon, both of which are objects of worship among primitive people. Tuesday took its name from Zeus; Wednesday from Woden; Thursday from Thor; Friday from Frigg, the wife of Odin; and Saturday from Saturn, the god of crops.

This suggests that one of the basic responsibilities of a Christian is to redeem his days from paganism.

88

All his time, whether at work or study or play, should be made to serve the God of love and truth and righteousness.

May my life be filled with rejoicing and gladness, O God, because I have made my time an offering to you. Give me direction and purpose in all that I do. Amen.

TUESDAY—Week 12

AN INCREASING CRIME   Read Ps. 90:1-12

So teach us to number our days that we may get a heart of wisdom.—Ps. 90:12

One of the words frequently used to describe a place to eat and drink is "lounge." In my city there is a Palace Lounge, a Cadillac Lounge, a Stadium Lounge, a Driftwood Lounge, and many others. They are symbols of an age in which lounging has become a favorite occupation. Lacking any sense of mission or deep concern for beauty and truth, people spend their time trying to overcome their boredom.

On a boat going down the Rhine River through a beautiful valley rich in history and legend, some American tourists sat on the deck playing cards. "There is the famous Lorelei Rock," someone called out. "So what?" said one of the Americans as they gave a passing glance at the fabled cliff and continued their game. Says Rebecca McCann:

> Some people speak of killing time,
> I don't know of any greater crime.
> With work and beauty they might fill it,
> But they sit around and kill it.

Instead of killing time, we need to learn how to fill it with positive values.

Dear God, you have placed me in an interesting world. Open my eyes to its beauty and joy. Keep me from ever being bored with life. Amen.

WEDNESDAY—Week 12

CLEAN FUN AND MEAN FUN   Read Matt. 27:27-31

And kneeling before him they mocked him, saying, "Hail, King of the Jews!"—Matt. 27:29

The Roman soldiers made fun of Jesus while they were waiting for him to be led away to his execution. Time hung heavy on their hands, and they were willing to do anything for the sake of a little sport. Stripping Jesus of his clothes, they arrayed him in an old purple robe, such as a king might once have worn. Then they put on his head a crown of thorns and took turns kneeling before him and saying, "Hail, King of the Jews." For Jesus it was humiliation and mental torture, but to the soldiers it was a diverting pastime.

One of the great dividing lines that cuts across varied forms of amusement is between clean fun and mean fun. Some people are so thoughtless in seeking their own pleasure that they become a source of harm or unhappiness to others. They take delight in tormenting a person they do not like and in committing acts of vandalism.

Every person needs fun and relaxation, but our good times ought never to mean pain to someone else. One standard by which to judge our leisure time activity is this: Is it a source of happiness and moral health to all who are affected by it?

Save me, O God, from ever trying to find happiness for myself in something that would make others unhappy. May I love my neighbor as myself. Amen.

MANSIONS MORE BEAUTIFUL THAN TAJ MAHAL
Read Matt. 15:32-39

Make love your aim.—1 Cor. 14:1

Most people who have been in India and have visited the Taj Mahal will agree that it is the most beautiful building they have ever seen. It was built by a Moslem ruler as a tomb for his favorite wife. When you stand at a little distance and gaze at it in the moonlight, it gleams with radiance.

The fact that people in India are so rightly proud of it gives added significance to an article in an Indian magazine which said, "Mansions more beautiful than Taj Mahal are arising in India." The writer told about a group of high school boys from Bombay who spent their vacation working nine hours a day without pay under a glaring Oriental sun to build a home for lepers. The article said: "While Taj Mahal was built for the dead, this has been a labor of love for the suffering members of our society, that they may have a happy place to live in."

"Mansions more beautiful than Taj Mahal!" They are built by love. Perhaps you can have a part in building them. In every country and every community there are people in need of help and worthy causes that are calling for leadership.

O God, make my life so full of love that it will overflow into the lives of others. May the world become more beautiful because of the love which I share. Amen.

ONLY GOD CAN RE-CREATE   Read Ps. 51:1-13

Create in me a clean heart, O God, and put a new and right spirit within me.—Ps. 51:10

The object of recreation is to *re-create*, to give a person fresh life and inner renewal. Since God is the Creator, one must allow himself to be molded and guided by God if he is to be made new.

Part of our leisure, then, needs to be used in a way that will help us to keep God at the center of our lives. Too often he is pushed out on the fringe. This is the reason that worship is so important and that part of Sunday should be reserved for this special purpose. Worship in its literal meaning is "worthship." It is acknowledging that ultimate worth, the values that really matter, has its source in God.

If spiritual values are not to be crowded out of life in our hurried age, regular opportunity must be given for their cultivation. The spirit, as well as the body, must have exercise or it grows flabby and weak. "What greater calamity can fall upon a people than loss of worship?" exclaimed Thomas Carlyle. That misfortune quickly comes upon those for whom the Sabbath day is a time only for television and pleasure-chasing. Sunday needs to include the re-creating of the spirit.

I thank you, O God, that I live in a country where each person is free to worship according to his own conscience. Grant that religious freedom may not lead me to religious neglect. Amen.

MAKING JESUS THE COMPANION OF OUR PLEASURES

Read John 2:1-11

Then the disciples were glad when they saw the Lord.
—John 20:20

The gospel of John pictures Jesus as one who made others glad by his presence. When he went to a wedding in Cana, he was key figure to the continued enjoyment of the festivities which followed it. An Oriental wedding was a joyous occasion which lasted for several days. After the ceremony, the bride and groom did not go away on a honeymoon, but were escorted to their home where they held an open house for their friends. Jesus' first miracle was that of turning water into wine so that people might keep on having a good time.

Another unforgettable scene came at the end of his ministry as described in the last chapter of John. After the disciples had spent all night fishing, he cooked breakfast for them around a campfire on the shore of Galilee. The New Testament makes it plain that Jesus was no killjoy. He knew how to have a good time.

Jesus seeks to be the companion of our pleasures as well as of our work and worship. One standard which a Christian can set up for his recreation is whether he is planning the kind of occasion at which Jesus would be glad to be present.

O God, I would learn to enjoy life in all its fullness. I pray that I may come to know Jesus as a friend who adds to the happiness of every occasion. In his name. Amen.

WINNING THE GAME OF LIFE

SUNDAY—Week 13

A CHAMPION FOR CHRIST   Read 1 Cor. 9:24-27
(Phillips)

You ought to run with your minds fixed on winning the prize—1 Cor. 9:24

If you are interested in the sports section of the Bible, turn to the ninth chapter of Paul's first letter to the church in Corinth. It is evident that Paul was fond of athletics and had attended many of the contests which were popular in his time. Doubtless he had witnessed the famous Olympic games which had been held in Greece since the eighth century before Christ. Listen to him in the Phillips translation as he urges his readers to run the race for Christ with the determination of an athlete to do his best to win the laurel crown:

"Do you remember how, on a racing track, every competitor runs, but only one wins the prize! Well, you ought to run with your minds fixed on winning the prize! Every competitor in athletic events goes into serious training. Athletes will take tremendous pains for a fading crown of leaves. But our contest is for an eternal crown that will never fade."

"I run the race then with determination. I am no shadow boxer. I really fight! I am my body's

sternest master, for fear that when I have preached
to others I should myself be disqualified."

To be a champion for Christ—the best possible
Christian! This is a great goal.

**Grant, O God, that I may know the joy of doing my
best. May I put myself under the discipline which will
enable me to do better tomorrow, and will keep me
striving toward an even higher goal. Amen.**

MONDAY—Week 13

PLAYING FAIR   Read 2 Tim. 2:1-5

**An athlete is not crowned unless he competes accord-
ing to the rules.—2 Tim. 2:5**

The most commonly accepted principle in games
and athletic contests is that one should play fair.
To cheat is considered contemptible. One should be
willing to go down to defeat rather than win by
breaking the rules. If a person refuses to obey the
rules, the person is put out of the game.

Abraham Lincoln once had a wrestling match
with a man named Armstrong who used tactics
that Lincoln considered unfair. Lincoln grabbed the
man with his long arms, lifted him off the ground
and shook him as he said: "Play fair, will you?
If you win, win! If you lose, lose, but do it like a
man!"

Sportsmanship provides a standard for life. No
one should ask for special favors which are not
allowed to other people. Everyone should have an
equal chance to show what he can do regardless of
the color of his skin or his family connections. This
is playing according to the golden rule. Says Grantland Rice:

When the One Great Scorer comes to write
    against your name,
He marks—not that you won or lost—
    but how you played the game.

Make me a person of honor, O God. Keep me from cheating or trying to evade the rules. Above everything else may I place the integrity of my own soul. Amen.

TUESDAY—Week 13

THE NECESSITY OF DISCIPLINE Read Heb. 12:5-11

For the moment all discipline seems painful rather than pleasant; later it yields the peaceful fruit of righteousness.—Heb. 12:11

The winning athlete is the person who puts himself under discipline. Avoiding every form of self-indulgence, he makes persistent efforts to build up his body and learn the needed techniques and skills. Whatever the cost in time and effort, he is willing to train and prepare.

In any high achievement, discipline is indispensable. Behind every act of superior ability in athletics, music, art or scholarship, you will find a willingness to accept training. It is not otherwise in the finest kind of moral and spiritual development. If a person takes the Christian life seriously, he will find time for prayer, Bible study, public worship, spiritual fellowship, and selfless service. A person may say he has no time for these matters, but without them he will never master the art of Christian living.

Jesus emphasized the need for self-denial and sacrifice. These are not for their own sakes but are the means of attaining a great purpose. Paul said the athlete strives for a "perishable wreath," but the Christian seeks one which is "imperishable."

96

The follower of Christ is seeking to develop a life and a society based on values that are eternal. The goal is worth the effort.

Eternal God, may I face the fact that there is no easy way to reach a high goal. Make me willing to do what I need to do even though it means effort and sacrifice. Amen.

WEDNESDAY—Week 13

FALLING FORWARD   Read Phil. 3:7-16

Forgetting what lies behind and straining forward to what lies ahead, I press on toward the goal.—Phil. 3:13-14

One of the early lessons learned by every football player is to fall forward when he is tackled while carrying the ball. That adds a few feet to the distance he has gained, and every yard counts. He is that much nearer the goal.

A player does not often get a chance to make a brilliant run for a long gain. For the most part, the ball is carried across the field by a series of failures to reach the goal line. Falling forward can be a decisive factor in final success.

The wise person learns to use failure so that it contributes to the advancement of his purpose. Perhaps you fall short of a passing mark in a course in school. Instead of becoming a dropout, you can make up your mind to study harder. That is falling forward. Or perhaps someone says something you do not like; you get mad and do something mean or unkind. You have fallen short of the goal of Christian self-control, but you are falling forward if you pick yourself up with the decision

97

to ask the person's forgiveness and master your temper. The Christian will learn from his mistakes and keep pressing on.

Dear Father, make me wise enough to profit by my failures. Save me from the temptation to be a quitter. May I have the courage to renew my efforts. Amen.

THURSDAY—Week 13

opening ✓

MAKING A SACRIFICE HIT   Read 1 John 3:11-18

By this we know love, that he laid down his life for us; and we ought to lay down our lives for the brethren. —1 John 3:16

Everyone who plays baseball knows what it means to make a sacrifice hit. The man at bat may long to take a big swing and try to knock out a home run, but for the sake of the team he does something different. He denies himself. The score is close and one man is on first base. The batter makes a bunt so that the runner on first can advance to second and be in a position to reach home if the next batter makes a hit. One man gives up his desire for a grandstand play in the hope of winning a victory for his team.

This is the spirit which has won repeated victories for the advancement of mankind. The greatest sacrifice hit ever made was by Jesus, who knew nothing about baseball but had an amazing knowledge of the game of life. He laid down his own life that other people might learn how to live more abundantly. He wanted people to understand the sacrificial love which is in the heart of God and ought to be in the hearts of men.

Jesus calls for followers who will play the game of life on his team.

98

Dear Father, give me the insight and courage that will enable me to take a sacrificial attitude toward life. May I know the joy of those who play on the team with Christ as their captain. Amen.

FRIDAY—Week 13

KEEP ON KEEPING ON   Read Luke 13:31-35

I must go on my way today and tomorrow and the day following.—Luke 13:33

A traveler in ancient Greece lost his way. He asked Socrates, who was sitting by the roadside, how to reach Mt. Olympus. "Just make every step you take go in that direction," replied Socrates. That is the only way that anyone will ever reach anyplace worth going. Keep your eye on the goal. Do not let anyone persuade you to make a detour. If people invite you to ride with them, be sure they are going toward the destination that you wish to reach.

A simple rule for adequate living is that one must be singleminded. All sorts of alluring things keep beckoning to us as we make the journey of life, and it is easy to turn aside from the one thing we most wish to accomplish.

When Nehemiah was leading the returned Jewish exiles in rebuilding the walls of Jerusalem, the enemies tried to entice him to leave his work and hold a conference with them on the plain. His reply was, "I am doing a great work and I cannot come down."

If you wish to win a game, you must play to win. No one can do his best if he is half-hearted.

Dear God, grant that I may keep my eyes on the one goal I most desire to reach. Instead of complaining about difficulties, may I do my best with what I have. Amen.

SATURDAY—Week 13

THE TORCH RACE OF THE CHRISTIAN

Read John 5:30-40

He was a burning and shining lamp.—John 5:35

The ancient Greeks had many athletic events which are not held in our own day. One was a race in which each runner carried a torch and was under the necessity of keeping it lighted while he ran. The winner was the one who arrived first at the goal with his torch still burning.

Although such a race is no longer a part of our athletics, it is always a part of the Christian life. Many people running toward the goal of material success are hailed by the world as winners, although they have failed to keep the torch of truth and honor lighted. Others have been so wrapped up in selfish pursuits that they have failed to do their parts toward creating a just and brotherly society. Instead of being considered winners, such people might more properly be called chiselers or parasites.

To be the most effective Christian, one needs a lighted personality so that he can act as a source of light to those around him. If he allows his light to go out, he is a dismal failure in the race for a higher life.

Dear God, help me to run with patience the race that is set before me, looking toward Jesus as my goal and my guide. If my light begins to flicker or grow dim, may I reach out to him as the Light of the world and renew my flame. Amen.

100

CHRISTIANS IN AN UNCHRISTIAN WORLD

SUNDAY—Week 14

CHRISTIANS IN AN UNCHRISTIAN WORLD
Read Phil. 4:10-23

All the saints greet you, especially those of Caesar's household.—Phil. 4:22

People who fail to be true to their inner convictions about right and wrong often excuse themselves by saying that it is impossible to be Christian in the kind of world in which we now live. We blame our inward failure on outward circumstances, and say the standards of Christ are too high to be practiced. Not wanting to be unpopular, we excuse ourselves for going along with the crowd.

It will strengthen our moral fiber if we remember the conditions under which Christianity had its birth and engaged in a winning struggle for existence. When the apostle Paul wrote a letter to the Philippians from Rome, he included a greeting from the saints in Caesar's household. Surely that was a difficult situation in which to be a follower of Christ! How could a man adhere to Christian principles if he were a servant in the palace of the pagan Nero? The sordidness and sensuality of life in first-century Rome far exceeded anything we know today.

If a person is to be a Christian in any age, he must do what the early Christians did. They developed the inner strength which enabled them to be Christian regardless of what others were doing.

Give me the courage, O God, to maintain the integrity of my own soul. Take away my fear of unpopularity and make me loyal to the best that I know. Amen.

MONDAY—Week 14

DRIFTING AWAY FROM CHRIST Read 2 Tim. 4:9-18

Demas, in love with this present world, has deserted me.—2 Tim. 4:10

Demas became a Christian, but found the Christian way of life so difficult that he gave it up. For a time he was associated with Paul and Luke. In one of his letters Paul refers to him as a fellow worker, but for some reason Demas' loyalty began to wane. Probably he failed to realize how difficult it would be to live by the spirit of love in a world of greed, and to remain pure in a world of sensuality.

It is easy to drift away from high standards without realizing what is happening. If a person rents a boat on the Jordan River and lets it go with the current instead of rowing, he will end in the Dead Sea. Something like that may have happened to Demas. To be a Christian in the first century meant that one had to pull hard against the influence of his environment. It has never been possible in any community or any age to drift into the Christian life.

Paul does not say that Demas became a bad man but merely that he loved the world as it already was. To be satisfied with life as it is—this is the great enemy of the Christian life.

102

Make me steadfast in my loyalty to you, O God. Keep me from drifting into some Dead Sea which is barren of life and hope. Amen.

TUESDAY—Week 14

BOWING TO THE IMAGE OF GOLD Read Dan. 3:1-18

But if not, be it known to you, O king, that we will not serve your gods or worship the golden image which you have set up.—Dan. 3:18

In one of the great stories of the Old Testament, three young Jews in Babylon were threatened with death in a fiery furnace if they refused to worship a golden image of the emperor. To have bowed before such an object was forbidden by the ten commandments. It would have violated the innermost sanctity of their souls, and they refused to conform to the king's decree. Haled before the monarch, they continued to make an unflinching refusal.

The three men were determined that they would not compromise. They decided that physical existence was a minor matter compared with loyalty to their deepest convictions. They believed that God would intervene in their behalf, but if not, they preferred to die and maintain their own self-respect rather than live like cowards.

The story is more than biblical history. An image of gold is set up in our modern Babylon and people bow down before it. "Give me money," they pray, "by fair means if it is possible, but by other means if necessary."

The question is, can we still refuse to sell our souls, even if it means being cast into the fiery furnace of poverty?

Father in heaven, grant that we may not be conformed to the standards of this world but be transformed by thy spirit within us. Amen.

WEDNESDAY—Week 14

THE CHRISTIAN'S REWARD   Read Dan. 3:19-30

Lo, I am with you always.—Matt. 28:20

The story of Shadrach, Meshach and Abednego has a significant conclusion. King Nebuchadnezzar, like a true dictator, kept his word. The three men were thrown into the fiery furnace. A little later the king peered into the fire to make sure that the flames had done their deadly work. He started back in astonishment. Turning to his courtiers, he asked, "Did we not cast three men bound into the furnace?" "True, O king," replied the attendants. And the king cried out, "But I see four men loose, walking in the midst of the fire, and they are not hurt; and the appearance of the fourth is like a son of the gods."

God does not always save his children from the fire, but he never leaves them alone. Those who are willing to suffer for their convictions are the ones who become supremely aware of the presence of a Divine Helper. This is the great reward of spiritual steadfastness. Give your first loyalty to God, and you will find God a living reality. God becomes the companion of those who are true to him. The final message of Christ to his followers is "Lo, I am with you always."

Dear Father God, whether my path leads me through green pastures and beside still waters, or through some fiery furnace, grant that I may have you as my companion and source of strength. Amen.

104

THURSDAY—Week 14

CONFORMITY AND INDEPENDENCE

Read 1 Pet. 2:11-17

Live as free men, yet without using your freedom as a pretext for evil.—1 Pet. 2:16

One of the confusing aspects of modern conformity is that so many people, in accepting the standards of their own particular crowd, do so in the name of personal liberty. They say they are freeing themselves from the worn-out ideas of the past. Young people today, however, do not need to worry about being bound down by inherited traditions. That is far from being their difficulty. Their problem is slavery to the present, with its quickly changing fashions.

Take such issues as drinking, using drugs, or sexual freedom. The person who wants to be free to do as he pleases makes fun of restricting standards as being old-fashioned. He conforms to the popular craze and then prides himself on his courage in becoming free. This is a completely distorted idea of independence, which historically has involved the determination to stand for what one believes to be right and true, regardless of consequences.

Martin Luther, for instance, when threatened with death if he did not recant, replied, "Here I stand. I cannot do otherwise. God help me." It is a far cry from that attitude to the kind of independence which justifies self-indulgence and calls it freedom.

Guide my feet by the light of thy truth, O God. Grant that the truth may set me free from the bondage of past tradition and of superficial thinking in my own day. Amen.

FRIDAY—Week 14

IN TUNE WITH THE ETERNAL   Read 2 Tim. 2:8-19

Do your best to present yourself to God as one approved, a workman who has no need to be ashamed. —2 Tim. 2:15

When Demosthenes, the great orator of ancient Greece, gave one of his addresses, he arranged to have a curtain at the rear of the platform. Back of it he placed a slave who was a master musician. This man, at the end of each eloquent flight of oratory, sounded a lower note that recalled the speaker to his original pitch lest his voice get out of control in his eagerness to please and sway the audience.

In our desire for the applause of the crowd, we are always in danger of forgetting the deeper note of Christian faith. Continually we are tempted to seek the acclaim of men instead of the approval of God. We tend to say, "I am only human and must not expect too much of myself." We need to be reminded of the words of John, "See what love the Father has bestowed upon us, that we should be called children of God."

What if to be human is to be a child of God? Man may be a bundle of conflicting desires, but his true self is the one which relates him to the divine. Each day we ought to tell ourselves anew that we belong to God.

Dear Father, help me to keep my life in tune with the eternal. May I never become deaf to thy voice as it seeks to call me back to my best self. In Jesus' name. Amen.

106

SATURDAY—Week 14

BLIND FOLLOWERS OF THE CROWD

Read Ex. 23:1-11

You shall not follow a multitude to do evil.—Ex. 23:2

In the mountains of Norway and Sweden can be found curious little mouselike animals called lemmings. The strange thing about them is that every few years they make a mass migration to the sea. They breed rapidly and, when the population has reached large numbers, they come together in crowds and start on what seems to be a search for more room. Taking the path of least resistance, they swarm down from the mountains into the valleys and keep going until they reach the ocean. Then they stream out into the water and are drowned.

You can excuse that kind of action in a lemming, but not in a man. Yet again and again we see people carried away by an unthinking crowd, none of whom knows where he is going. One person does a thing, another acts in exactly the same way, and soon a new craze is started, although the members of the unthinking herd seem not to know where they are headed or what the result will be.

Jesus calls to us all and says "Follow me." But he wants us to understand the meaning of Christian discipleship. He asks us to love him with our minds as well as our hearts.

Save me, O God, from being lost in the crowd. May I think my own thoughts, make my own decisions, and keep my eyes on Christ. Amen.

LOVE NEVER FAILS

SUNDAY—Week 15

THE CREATIVE POWER OF LOVE   Read 1 Cor. 13

Love never fails.—1 Cor. 13:8 (KJV)

In the greatest passage in the writings of the apostle Paul, he said that love never fails. This sounds like an exaggeration. People are often cynical about love and consider it too sentimental a basis on which to built a stable society. But listen to Napoleon Bonaparte, who was one of the greatest exponents of force the world has ever known:

"Do you know what amazes me more than all else? The impotence of force to organize anything. There are only two powers in the world, the spirit and the sword. In the long run, the spirit will always conquer the sword."

More recently, Arnold Toynbee, the great British historian, has insisted that love is the only creative force in history. He quotes Jesus' command, "Love your enemies and do good to those who hate you." Then he adds, "Literal obedience to these words has become the only practical alternative to mass suicide."

What can the ordinary person do to help make love a stronger force in the world? He can at least light a candle in the darkness. He can demonstrate its meaning in his own life and give his support to organized efforts which are working toward this goal.

Forgive us, O God, that we have been so slow to believe in this power of love. Lead us into a clearer understanding of the nature of the universe in which we live. Amen.

MONDAY—Week 15

GOD IS LOVE   Read 1 John 4:1-8

He who does not love does not know God; for God is love.—1 John 4:98

Years ago I sat on the porch of a Naples hotel with a party of American tourists. It was late evening and objects were dimly visible as we looked over the bay. We were talking about our disappointment in not being able to take an anticipated trip up the side of Mt. Vesuvius. The road to the mountain was closed because there had been faint rumblings which indicated that the volcano might become active.

Suddenly the whole area was brightly illuminated by a burst of flames from the volcano. Before, we had seen indistinctly in the darkness. Now everything stood out clearly with a beauty that could never be forgotten. Something deep within the earth had been released and everything had a different appearance.

It is the Christian conviction that in Christ we see the inner nature of the universe. In him was revealed the light and power of the divine love which puts us in harmony with the eternal.

God is love. This is the reason that patient, long-suffering, and sacrificial love never fails. A new day will dawn for mankind when people express this conviction in all their relationships with each other.

Brighten my life, O God, with an awareness of thy love. Because Christ is the light of my own life, may I be able to brighten the world around me. In Jesus' name. Amen.

TUESDAY—Week 15

THE NEW COMMANDMENT   Read John 13:31-35

A new commandment I give to you, that you love one another; even as I have loved you.—John 13:34

One reason for our difficulty in understanding Jesus' teaching about love is that we use the word in a general way to cover many different kinds of experiences. We speak of a man's love for his wife, his children, and his country. Then we use the same word to describe his attitude toward his dog, his automobile, or his golf game. The phrase "I just love it" is applied to almost everything.

The Greeks were more precise. They had three different words for love. One was "eros" which is the natural magnetism between the sexes. A second was "philia" which means friendship. The third word for love was "agape" which is the self-giving love of God himself. It is hardly found outside the New Testament. A love such as God revealed to Christ was so unique that it took a new Greek word to describe it.

Agape is the sort of love which seeks to help other people regardless of the inconvenience and sacrifice. It suffers long and is kind and does not draw back from the cross. This kind of love has only one source. It comes to us when our lives are fully open to God.

110

Dear Father, teach us the meaning of love at its deepest level. May our hearts have so much of your spirit that we give ourselves gladly to meet human need. Amen.

WEDNESDAY—Week 15

REMEMBERED FOR HER LOVE Read Matt. 20:20-28

Whoever would be great among you must be your servant.—Matt. 20:26

Few people today could tell the cause of the Crimean war which took place in the middle of the nineteenth century. Most persons could not even give the names of the countries engaged in it. Everyone, however, knows the name of Florence Nightingale, whose love for sick and wounded soldiers made her share their suffering.

Born into a wealthy family, she was not satisfied to sit idly at home and do nothing but have a good time. Against the opposition of her parents, who objected to having their daughter do menial work, she studied to be a nurse. When news came from the Crimea about the terrible suffering among the ill and injured soldiers, she organized a band of nurses and established a hospital at Scutari. By her skill and love, she revolutionized army nursing. Her work was the forerunner of the Red Cross, and she will always be remembered as one of the great women of history.

A love which identifies itself with the needs of suffering people never fails to win their gratitude and never fails to ennoble the life of the person who practices it.

Dear Father, give me the courage and willingness to enter the door which opens to human need. May my life

111

be the means by which thy love, with its healing influence, is made available to the world. For Jesus' sake. Amen.

THURSDAY—Week 15

EXTREMES OF LOVE   Read Luke 23:32-43

Love bears all things, believes all things, hopes all things, endures all things.—1 Cor. 13:7

One of the little-known men among the pioneers of Christian missions was Bartholomew Ziegenbalg, who went to the Danish colony of Tranquebar in India in 1705. He responded to an appeal made by the King of Denmark, but was at first bitterly opposed by commercial leaders. They were afraid that his religious work would interfere with their profits. Through their influence he was arrested by colonial authorities and put in a dungeon.

When threatened with extreme physical punishment, Ziegenbalg replied, "I too will proceed to extremes—of love." After his release from prison, he learned the Tamil language and translated the New Testament so that the story of Jesus might be available to the natives in their own tongue.

The secret of his life was his willingness to go to extremes of love. He was ready to endure any kind of hardship for the sake of showing his love to the Tamil people. His Christlike life enabled them to understand the love of God as it had been made known in the life and teachings of Jesus. It is a love like this, which goes to extremes, that finally succeeds when everything else has failed.

O God, we pray for a love which is so strong and

steadfast that it can endure all things. Keep us from faltering and quitting when love grows difficult. Amen.

FRIDAY—Week 15

ANIMALS RESPOND TO LOVE   Read Luke 6:27-36

Love is patient and kind.—1 Cor. 13:4

Ivan Tors, famous film producer and wild animal trainer, says that one of the lessons he has learned in his work with animals is the power of love. He is sure that "the silent language of the heart" can break down the barriers that ordinarily exist between men and beasts. "Our whole approach to working with animals," he says, "all our training methods, all our results, are based on affection. Human beings need a certain amount of love if they're to develop into normal, friendly, unantagonistic people. It is the same with animals, too."

At his animal ranch, the trainers never use any kind of physical punishment and never do anything that would incite the animals' fear. The main job of the ranch workers is to pet the animals and make them feel that they are surrounded by love.

Does not this give us fresh insight into the basic power of love? We have relied mainly on force and fear as the means by which we try to turn bad people into good members of society. Force may restrain people from doing wrong, but it never changes a bad person into a good one. This happens only through love.

Dear God, help us to realize the transforming power that our lives can exert over other people. Save us from selfishness and give us a steadfast love for those around us. Amen.

THE UNDYING INFLUENCE OF LOVE

Read 1 John 4:13-21

This commandment we have from him, that he who loves God should love his brother also.—1 John 4:21

One of the simplest and most profound prayers of the Christian faith has come down to us from the thirteenth century. It was written by Francis of Assisi. The son of a prosperous businessman, he led a gay and carefree youth until he had a vision of Christ, which started him upon the quest for a Christlike life. Dedicating himself to a career of poverty and Christian love, he became the founder of the San Franciscan order which became a saving influence in the church and in society. This was his prayer:

Lord, make me an instrument of Thy peace; where there is hatred, let me sow love; where there is doubt, faith; where there is despair, hope; where there is darkness, light; where there is sadness, joy.
O Divine Master, grant that I may not so much seek to be consoled as to console; to be understood as to understand; to be loved as to love; for it is in giving that we receive; it is in forgiving that we are forgiven; and it is in dying that we are born into Eternal Life. Amen.

Love never fails to have an undying influence when it comes from a life as sincere and unselfish as that of Francis of Assisi.

Thank you, O God, for the great souls who have shown mankind the simplicity and beauty of Christian love. Deliver me from the bitterness and cynicism which is so widespread in our day. In Jesus' name. Amen.

EXPLORING WITH GOD

SUNDAY—Week 16

ENLARGING OUR IDEA OF GOD   Read Ps. 93

O Lord, our Lord, how majestic is thy name in all the earth.—Ps. 8:1

Science has rendered a great service to religious faith. Through it we have come to an enlarged conception of the greatess and glory of God. No longer can we believe in a little God. He is not simply the God of the earth, but the ruler of the universe.

Dr. John H Martin, physicist at the Argonne National Laboratory of the Atomic Energy Commission, says that he has never encountered a scientist who does not believe in some kind of higher power. In a great testimony to his faith, he says: "My respect and admiration of God's handiwork grows with every passing day I spend in this laboratory." The trouble with the religious thinking of many people is that their ideas of God are too small and restricted. Their God is not big enough to include all aspects of life.

A mother was reading Bible stories to her daughter when the girl looked up and said, "God must have been exciting in those days." "Yes, he was," replied the mother, "but if you try to learn about him and obey him, you will find him even more exciting today."

Almighty God, you have been the hope of ages past. May we still find our hope in thee for years to come. May we come to know you better and love you more as we live in obedience to your will. Amen.

MONDAY—Week 16

WHERE IS GOD GOING?   Read Deut. 30:11-20

I have set before you life and death, blessing and curse; therefore choose life, that you and your descendants may live.—Deut. 30:19

William E. Gladstone, when Prime Minster of England, said the great question for statesmen was where God was going in the next fifty years. Evidently the national leaders of his day failed to find the answer, for the next half-century brought the First World War with its holocaust of hate.

Where is God going? An intelligent Christian ought to know the answer. He is going in the direction pointed out by Christ. His goal is a civilization in which people live together in a brotherhood of peace and unity. There is new hope today for such a kingdom. Greed and selfishness have shown how terrible their results can be. With new humility, men are seeking a solution to their predicament.

Young people need to do more than protest against the past. They must explore the ways in which men can be saved from their selfishness and led forward into a new day. Says Christopher Fry:

> Affairs are now soul size.
> The enterprise
> Is exploration into God.

O God, we pray that you will make us adequate for

the opportunities that are ours. May our human efforts be in harmony with your purpose for the world and for our personal lives. Amen.

TUESDAY—Week 16

TRUSTING GOD'S GUIDANCE   Read Isa. 58:1-11

The Lord will guide you continually.—Isa. 58:11

Birds and animals have a surprising ability to find their way over long distances. By some instinctive sense of direction, they seem to know the way to go. Dogs have returned home after being carried hundred of miles away. Birds migrate to the south for winter and return to their former habitat in the spring.

A young man left his home in New England to make his way in the world. Uncertain about his future, he was anxious and lonely. It was the autumn of the year, and he saw a wild duck flying south. He began to think about the way a bird, by following a divinely implanted instinct, was able to fly unerringly to its goal. The conviction came to him that his own life could have heavenly guidance if he were ready to follow the direction of the divine will. Out of that experience came William Cullen Bryant's poem, "To a Waterfowl," which ends with the lines:

He who, from zone to zone
Guides through the boundless sky thy certain flight,
In the long way that I must tread alone,
Will lead my steps aright.

We thank you, O God, that not even a bird falls to the ground without thy notice, and that our lives are precious in thy sight. Make me willing to accept the guidance you are always trying to give. Amen.

WEDNESDAY—Week 16

CHRIST LEADS US IN TRIUMPH Read Heb. 11:1-16

Thanks be to God, who in Christ always leads us in triumph.—2 Cor. 2:14

The words "advent" and "adventure" are so closely related that they cannot be separated. They suggest that the advent of Jesus into any person's life will start him on a new adventure. Too often we think of religion as dull and boring. But if we take our Christian faith seriously, it will give life a finer flavor and make it more exciting.

For one thing, it will stir us to set the house of our inner lives in order. This is no small undertaking. It means wrestling with the evil spirits that constantly seek to control our hearts. We will never be satisfied until we have triumphed over them.

More than that, if we follow Christ, we will find him leading us in a campaign against the forces that oppose his kingdom of love. We will no longer be satisfied to turn our backs on the injustice around us while we search for a little more money or try to amuse ourselves.

Read the story of the New Testament Christians. As new men in Christ, they were on a crusade for a new world. "Christ leads us in triumph," said Paul. Turn your life over to Christ and you too can have an adventurous and triumphant experience.

O God, grant that I may keep my eyes fixed on Jesus and that I may see the full glory of the Christian life. Help me to show what it means to be his follower and to have some part in winning a victory for his kingdom. Amen.

STEADFAST OBEDIENCE TO GOD   Read Ps. 57

**My heart is steadfast, O God, my heart is steadfast!
—Ps. 57:7**

When the French army collapsed in the Second
World War and Paris was occupied by Nazi soldiers,
a group of Christian students met to reaffirm their
religious faith. They expressed their confidence in
the future by sending a two-word cablegram to a
society of Christian students in London. It said,
"God reigns." Through a mistake in the transmitting
of the message, the words received in London were
"God resigns." The English group immediately wired
back the reply: "Decision regretted. British policy
remains the same."

Many people have been saying that God is dead.
Others seem to think that he has resigned or, at
least, is no longer active in the world he created.
People are needed who will remain steadfast and
live in continued obedience to God as he has made
himself known in the life and teachings of Christ.

Great Christians who have lived in an intimate
relationship with God have found that he becomes
more real to them in their time of deepest need.
St. Augustine, in the turbulent days when the Roman Empire was breaking up, asserted his faith
by saying, "God never forsakes a man unless he is
first forsaken by him." That is a sustaining conviction which is needed for our own day.

**Dear God, help us to deepen our religious convictions.
Enlighten us when we are perplexed, strengthen us when
we are weak, and give us courage when we are afraid.
Amen.**

FRIDAY—Week 16

OUR SECURITY IS GOD Read Rom. 8:31-39

I am sure that neither death, nor life, . . . nor anything else in all creation, will be able to separate us from the love of God.—Rom. 8:38-39

One of the most persistent explorers of the Arctic Ocean was an adventurous sea captain by the name of Sir John Franklin. In 1818 he was chosen to command the *Trent,* one of the three ships sent by the British admiralty to discover a Northwest passage to the Pacific Ocean. The expedition was unsuccessful and he was chosen to head another effort the following year. His party was gone for three and a half years, suffered incredible hardships and traveled over 1100 miles on snowshoes in the biting cold.

Before he started on the third trip which cost him his life, he made a revised map of the world. On it he charted some of his new information, but the most significant aspect of the map was religious. Cartographers had been accustomed to marking unknown territory with phrases such as: "Here be dragons"; "Here be demons"; "Here be sirens." Franklin did away with all thse phrases expressing fear and dread. In places where no exploration had yet been made, he wrote, "Here be God."

Write that over all the unexplored areas of your life. Wherever a Christian goes or whatever he does, he should have the faith that his life can be guided and guarded by God.

Strengthen my faith in your power and goodness, dear God. Help me to commit myself completely to your guidance and care. In Christ's name. Amen.

WHEN GOD IS REFUSED ADMISSION

Read Luke 9:51-56

Behold, I stand at the door and knock; if any one hears my voice and opens the door, I will come in to him.—Rev. 3:20

When a Samaritan village showed an unwillingness to have Jesus as its guest, he quietly passed it by. James and John were so angry that they wanted him to call down fire from heaven and destroy its inhospitable people. Jesus rebuked his hot-tempered disciples and led them on to another city.

This is typical of what Jesus is always doing. He never goes where he is not wanted. He knocks at the hearts of men and gently makes it known that he is willing to enter. When they refuse him, he quietly goes away.

The Samaritans never knew what they had missed. Sick persons might have been healed. Discouraged people might have been given new life. Sinful people might have been delivered from the bondage of their evil habits.

God's most terrible judgment may be, not in some dreaded punishment, but in what does not happen. Your life could become a life-giving stream, but it remains a little pool of stagnant water. Let God into your life and he will make it what it was intended to be. He will save you from littleness and lethargy and make you a channel through which his love can flow out into the world.

Forgive me, O God, for refusing to give you admission into my life. Awaken my soul to a knowledge of its loss, so that with shame and sorrow I may open wide the door. Amen.

WHO, ME?

SUNDAY—Week 17

PUT YOUR NAME DOWN   Read Acts 4:13-22

When they saw the boldness of Peter and John, . . . they recognized that they had been with Jesus.—Acts 4:13

During the latter part of the third century, when Christians were being fiercely persecuted, a young man named Adrian was a member of the Praetorian Guard. He had served with distinction and stood high in the favor of his officers.

Believing that Christians were a menace to the unity of the Roman empire, he was zealous in hunting them out and bringing them to trial. As he watched them suffer torture without wavering in their loyalty to Christ, he was stirred with admiration. Never before had he seen such heroism. He asked one of the Christians, "What gives you such strength and joy in the midst of your suffering?" "Our Lord Jesus Christ in whom we believe," was the reply.

Adrian began to have a secret longing for the kind of faith that could give such inner satisfaction. Finally he went to the judge in charge of the trials. "Put my name down, sir," he said. "I too am a Christian."

122

In America we have religious freedom. No one is persecuted for his faith, but it takes a brave commitment to be steadfastly true to your deepest convictions. Are you willing to put your name down as a Christian?

Dear Father in Heaven, make me a fearless follower of Jesus Christ. Regardless of what others may say or do, may I be loyal to him. For his sake. Amen.

MONDAY—Week 17

SAYING YES TO GOD   Read Isa. 6

Then I said, "Here I am! Send me."—Isa. 6:8

The days of Isaiah's youth were a time of prosperity and national expansion. An ambitious king by the name of Uzziah had enlarged the boundaries of Israel and forced the bordering tribes to pay tribute. The nation was enjoying a superficial prosperity and was smugly complacent.

Suddenly Uzziah was smitten with leprosy and died. The national outlook became confused and uncertain. War seemed imminent. Isaiah felt that what had happened was the judgment of God upon the nation's actions.

Going into the temple to pray, he had a vision of the holiness of God. It made him aware of the sinfulness of his own life and that of the nation.

As he sought cleansing and forgiveness for himself, he had a deeper insight into the nation's need for moral renewal. He knew that someone must protest against the course the nation was following. Someone must challenge the people to face the truth. The voice of God asked him the pointed question, "Whom shall I send and who will go for us?" "Here am I," answered Isaiah. "Send me."

123

The world today needs people who will be brave enough to speak the truth about national and international relationships.

Open my eyes, O God, that I may behold the glory of your righteousness. Take away my deafness that I may clearly hear your message, and give me the courage to be the messenger of your truth. Amen.

TUESDAY—Week 17

HOW MUCH DO I CARE? Read Gal. 6:1-10

Bear ye one another's burdens, and so fulfil the law of Christ.—Gal. 6:2

Albert Schweitzer spent his early life in a poor community on the edge of the Alps where his father was pastor. One day at school Albert defeated another boy in a wrestling match. Later he overheard him say, "If I had broth every day as the pastor's son has, I would be so strong he couldn't throw me." Albert decided he would not accept privileges for himself that were denied to others. He told his parents that he would not eat any more broth as long as there were boys who couldn't have any.

As Schweitzer grew older, he became a man with such a brilliant and disciplined mind that he achieved fame as a university professor, a writer, and a musician. Yet he could not remain satisfied to enjoy his personal success while people all over the world were suffering from poverty and disease. He studied to be a doctor and opened a hospital in the jungle of Africa.

The life of Schweitzer suggests questions we all must answer. To what extent are we justified in enjoying the good things of life that others cannot share? And how can a person most effectively help underprivileged people?

Dear Father, cleanse my heart of all selfish ambition. Enlarge my vision and give me a greater concern for the world's need. Grant that my life may become the doorway through which a healing ministry flows out into the lives of others. Amen.

WEDNESDAY—Week 17

GOD REFUSES TO ACCEPT EXCUSES
Read Ex. 4:10-17

Oh, my Lord, send, I pray, some other person.
—Ex. 4:13

Moses, while living in the royal palace of Egypt as the adopted son of the princess, made a rash attempt to help a Hebrew slave. As a result, he was forced to flee to Midian. There he was fortunate enough to marry the daughter of a wealthy shepherd. He had a comfortable and secure life with no worry about the future.

One day Moses became vividly aware of the presence of God who spoke to him out of a burning bush. "Come," he said, "I will send you to Pharaoh that you may bring forth my people, the sons of Israel, out of Egypt." Moses replied that he did not have the ability for such a difficult task. He asked God to send someone else. But God insisted that Moses should go. He would not accept any of Moses' excuses.

Perhaps you, too, are enjoying an easy, self-satisfied life. If you listen, you will hear God calling you to help some of the people who are victims of prejudice or poverty, or who suffer some other handicap.

125

In spite of all your excuses, God will keep on speaking until you answer the call.

Dear God, speak to me so plainly that I cannot fail to understand what you want me to do. Keep me from offering excuses. Make me willing to obey. Amen.

THURSDAY—Week 17

ANYONE CAN LIGHT A CANDLE Read Matt. 5:13-16

Let your light so shine before men, that they may see your good works and give glory to your Father who is in heaven.—Matt. 5:16

A pageant was once given in the Los Angeles coliseum which culminated in a unique lighting ceremony that made a deep impression on all who were present. The program director introduced it by saying: "Perhaps you sometimes tell yourself that your job isn't important because it is such a little job. But you are wrong. The most obscure person can be very important. Let me show you what I mean." Then he asked to have the lights turned off.

While the big auditorium was in complete darkness, the speaker struck a match. In the blackness everyone could see a tiny flame. "You can all see the importance of one little light," continued the director. "Now let everyone strike a match." All who had matches quickly responded and a gasp of surprise was heard throughout the vast audience. People were amazed at the total illumination which had been created. It was plainly evident that each little light helped to create the result.

"It is better to light a candle than to curse the darkness," says an old proverb. The world will be a little better or a little worse because of each individual.

Forgive me, O God, if I ever think my life is so unimportant that it doesn't matter what I do. Help me to brighten the corner where I am by reflecting the light of Christ from my own life. Amen.

FRIDAY—Week 17

TAKING UP THE CROSS   Read Luke 9:18-25

If any man would come after me, let him deny himself and take up his cross daily and follow me.—Luke 9:23

No symbol of the Christian faith has so much meaning as the cross. It speaks to us of a God who loves us so deeply that he enters into our human experiences and is willing to suffer for the sake of winning us to a higher life. It is composed of an upright column supporting a horizontal crossbeam. The upright reminds us that a person should be reaching up toward God in response to the divine love which reaches down to him. The crossbeam bids us remember that the one who feels the pull of God's love will reach out toward his fellowmen.

The horizontal is held in place by the upright. This stands for the great truth that our outward reach toward those who need our help is sustained by our upreach toward God. If we forget God's love for mankind, we will be less ready to deny ourselves for the sake of helping others.

An old hymn reminds us that the cross is for the disciple as well as for his Lord:

> Must Jesus bear the cross alone
> and all the world go free?
> No, there's a cross for everyone,
> and there's a cross for me.

Eternal Father, may the cross ever speak to me of thy love and make me ashamed of my own littleness. Give me the courage to walk in the way of the cross. May it be for me the way of life and peace. Amen.

127

A MAN SENT FROM GOD   Read John 1:1-7

There was a man sent from God, whose name was John.—John 1:6

John was as common a name in first-century Palestine as it is today in our own country. The Bible tells us not only about John the Baptist, but John the beloved disciple, and John Mark, who wrote the second book of the New Testament. Not only John but people with all sorts of names have been used by God to achieve his objectives. Dare then to believe that God has placed you in the world for a purpose, that he seeks to make you a fellow worker with himself, and to use you in helping to develop a world which can truly be called his kingdom.

The person who accepts life as a divine trust will find that it puts new meaning and glory into his existence. God is dependent on us. He has created his world in such a way that we have a responsibility for its welfare and progress. The eternal plans of God cannot be fulfilled without our help.

There was a man sent from God whose name was ———. The sentence is incomplete. Write your own name in the blank space. Then seek to make yourself worthy of God's faith in you.

Who, Me? Yes, You!

"Thy kingdom come, thy will be done on earth as it is in heaven." Grant that the prayer of Jesus may be my prayer. May I do my part in making heaven on earth. Amen.